100 Favorite Hymns

Stacy Edwards

THOMAS NELSON
Since 1798

Published in Nashville, Tennessee, by Thomas Nelson. Thomas Nelson is a registered trademark of HarperCollins Christian Publishing, Inc.

Thomas Nelson titles may be purchased in bulk for educational, business, fund-raising, or sales promotional use. For information, please email SpecialMarkets@ThomasNelson.com.

Unless otherwise noted, Scripture quotations are taken from the New King James Version®. © 1982 by Thomas Nelson. Used by permission. All rights reserved.

Scripture quotations marked NIV are from the Holy Bible, New International Version®, NIV®. Copyright © 1973, 1978, 1984, 2011 by Biblica, Inc.® Used by permission of Zondervan. All rights reserved worldwide. www.zondervan.com. The "NIV" and "New International Version" are trademarks registered in the United States Patent and Trademark Office by Biblica, Inc.®

Any internet addresses, phone numbers, or company or product information printed in this book are offered as a resource and are not intended in any way to be or to imply an endorsement by Thomas Nelson, nor does Thomas Nelson vouch for the existence, content, or services of these sites, phone numbers, companies, or products beyond the life of this book.

ISBN 978-1-4002-1-8998 (Hardcover)
ISBN 978-4002-1-9001 (eBook)

Printed in India

21 22 23 24 25 BPI 12 11 10 9 8 7 6 5 4 3

CONTENTS

Introduction 6

1. Higher Ground 9
2. Alas! and Did My Savior Bleed 11
3. All Creatures of Our God and King 13
4. My Hope Is Built on Nothing Less 15
5. My Jesus, I Love Thee. 17
6. O for a Thousand Tongues to Sing 19
7. More About Jesus. 21
8. Turn Your Eyes upon Jesus. 23
9. Just as I Am 25
10. What a Friend We Have in Jesus. 27
11. I Love to Tell the Story. 29
12. Take My Life, and Let It Be 31
13. I've Got Peace Like a River 33
14. Tell Me the Story of Jesus. 35
15. There Is a Balm in Gilead 37
16. He Keeps Me Singing 39
17. Immortal, Invisible, God Only Wise 41
18. Beulah Land. 43
19. Rescue the Perishing 45
20. Count Your Blessings 47
21. From All That Dwell Below the Skies 49
22. Are You Washed in the Blood?. 51
23. This Is My Father's World 53
24. Who Is He in Yonder Stall 55
25. The Old Rugged Cross. 57
26. There Is a Fountain 59
27. In the Garden 61
28. Softly and Tenderly 63
29. Leaning on the Everlasting Arms 65
30. Rock of Ages 67

31. It Is Well with My Soul 69
32. Jesus Loves Me 71
33. 'Tis So Sweet to Trust in Jesus 73
34. There Shall Be Showers of Blessing 75
35. Stand Up, Stand Up for Jesus 77
36. Onward, Christian Soldiers 79
37. When the Roll Is Called Up Yonder 81
38. There's a Land That Is Fairer Than Day 83
39. On Jordan's Stormy Banks I Stand 85
40. I Stand Amazed in the Presence 87
41. I'd Rather Have Jesus 89
42. The Love of God 91
43. Love Lifted Me 93
44. Tell It to Jesus 95
45. Blessed Assurance 97
46. The Lily of the Valley 99
47. Jesus Paid It All 101
48. I Know Whom I Have Believed 103
49. I Need Thee Every Hour 105
50. Jesus Is the Sweetest Name I Know 107
51. Redeemed, How I Love to Proclaim It 109
52. Lord, I Want to Be a Christian 111
53. Grace Greater Than Our Sin 113
54. O Happy Day That Fixed My Choice 115
55. O Worship the King 117
56. One Day 119
57. Make Me a Blessing 121
58. Pass Me Not, O Gentle Savior 123
59. Praise God, from Whom All Blessings Flow . . 125
60. Shall We Gather at the River 127
61. When We All Get to Heaven 129
62. Tell Me the Old, Old Story 131
63. Oh, How I Love Jesus 133
64. Send the Light 135
65. O Come, All Ye Faithful 137

66. No, Not One 139
67. Were You There 141
68. Since Jesus Came into My Heart 143
69. Trust and Obey 145
70. Crown Him with Many Crowns. 147
71. When I Survey the Wondrous Cross 149
72. Amazing Grace 151
73. Holy, Holy, Holy 153
74. Be Thou My Vision 155
75. Give Me Jesus 157
76. God Moves in a Mysterious Way 159
77. Wonderful Peace. 161
78. Breathe on Me. 163
79. I Will Sing of the Mercies of the Lord 165
80. Away in a Manger 167
81. Great Is Thy Faithfulness 169
82. Come, Thou Almighty King 171
83. Take Up Your Cross 173
84. We'll Understand It Better By and By 175
85. I've Got the Joy, Joy, Joy, Joy. 177
86. Have Thine Own Way, Lord. 179
87. It Came Upon the Midnight Clear 181
88. Stand by Me 183
89. I Remember Calvary 185
90. Open My Eyes, That I May See 187
91. Silent Night, Holy Night. 189
92. For All the Saints 191
93. I Have a Hope 193
94. Joy to the World 195
95. Master of the Sea 197
96. Jesus Is All the World to Me 199
97. I Must Tell Jesus. 201
98. Come, Thou Fount of Every Blessing 203
99. I Surrender All 205
100. This Little Light of Mine 207

INTRODUCTION

"Good hymns are an immense blessing to the Church. They train people for heaven, where praise is one of the principal occupations."
—J. C. RYLE

Hymns have the power to evoke specific memories. Whenever I hear "Just as I Am," for instance, I am back in the little church of my youth, reaching across the aisle to take hold of Mr. Page's hand at the close of our Sunday service. At the sound of "As the Deer," I imagine my wedding day and all of the hope and happiness it held. No doubt that you also have songs that take you back to a certain place in time.

There is something about a hymn that speaks to the deepest part of a person. It's been said that when someone is happy, he enjoys the music. But when sad, he understands the lyrics. Songs have a way of meeting us where we are and reminding us that, somewhere along the way, someone else has experienced or felt the very same things. There is, as Solomon stated, nothing new under the sun, and that is often a source of comfort.

Whether you grew up singing "I've Got the Joy, Joy, Joy, Joy down in My Heart" or "The Old Rugged Cross," hymns are timeless and continue to speak to people throughout the years. Some of the songs mentioned in this book are hundreds of years old, and yet the feelings come through just as strongly now as they did to the original singers. That is the power of a hymn. Let the music begin!

Thank You, Father, for these hymns that have been preserved for us throughout history. Help us to continue to sing these songs of praise and worship as expressions of our love for You. May the words of these songs keep our hearts and minds tuned to You.

1

I'm pressing on the
upward way,

New *heights* I'm
gaining ev'ry day;

Still praying as I
onward bound,

"Lord, plant my feet
on higher *ground*."

HIGHER GROUND

John Oatman Jr.'s hymn "Higher Ground" is a call to every believer to seek a more mature faith and a deeper connection with the Lord. Although he wrote around three thousand songs, "Higher Ground" has been a favorite since it was first published in 1898, perhaps because it puts into words a desire shared by followers of Christ throughout the years—to know Him more intimately and to follow Him more closely. It accurately describes the ideal course our faith would take as we mature in Christ.

Whether he was writing to the Philippians (3:21) or the Colossians (3:2), Paul often used the imagery of growing up, reaching for higher things, or moving upward when he wrote of his personal faith journey. It's like an old preacher once told me during a discussion on faith and prayer: "Our faith," he said, "is always either growing or shrinking; it's never stagnant." Paul's encouragement was to always be pressing on toward the prize and to seek the things that are above.

When it comes right down to it, John Oatman, the apostle Paul, and the old preacher were all seeking the same thing. They were seeking more of God. They desired more of His power and presence in their lives. May that be our aim as well. Let's seek a deeper faith. Make our love more sincere. Strive to know Him more. Plant our feet on higher ground.

Lord, help us to have faith that is constantly growing
and maturing. Give us a desire for more of You.

2

Alas! and did
my Savior bleed

And did my
Sov'reign die?

Would He devote
that *sacred* head

For such a
worm as I?

ALAS! AND DID MY SAVIOR BLEED

I am guilty of overanalyzing and making things far more complicated than is necessary. I've noticed we often do this when sharing the gospel with someone. Perhaps it's because we feel the weight of what is at stake, or maybe it's because we don't know when we'll have another opportunity to share with a particular person. Either way, the simplicity of the message is sometimes lost.

When Isaac Watts wrote "Alas! and Did My Savior Bleed," he had no way of knowing the impact it would have on a woman named Fanny Crosby. Crosby would become one of the most well-known hymnists by writing more than eight thousand songs in her lifetime. It is said that, at the age of thirty, she went to the altar during a church service and the congregation began singing Watts's hymn. Although she had been to the altar before, something about the words of this hymn resonated with her, and she surrendered her life to Jesus.

The essence of the gospel is that God took on flesh and died for "worms" like us. I can't help but wonder if it was that simple truth, written poetically through the pen of Watts, that penetrated Crosby's heart. That was certainly the message that Paul shared when, in his letter to Timothy, he wrote, "This *is* a faithful saying and worthy of all acceptance, that Christ Jesus came into the world to save sinners, of whom I am chief" (1 Timothy 1:15).

Lord, help us to share the gospel with simplicity
and sincerity. May we never lose sight of
the sacrifice You made for sinners.

3

All *creatures*
of our God and King,

Lift up your *Voice*
and with us sing,

Alleluia! *Alleluia!*

ALL CREATURES OF OUR GOD AND KING

Based on a poem written in 1225 by St. Francis of Assisi, William Draper wrote this universal call to praise we now know as "All Creatures of Our God and King." Draper altered the wording and set it to music for a children's program taking place at his church in the early 1900s. The hymn invites all of creation to praise its Creator. The sun, moon, wind, and clouds are all invited to express their adoration to the One who spoke them into existence.

The inspiration for the original work by St. Francis was Psalm 148. The parallels are obvious as the psalmist called on all of creation to praise the Lord. Everything from the highest heavens to the depths of the seas was called out—from flying birds to creeping things and everything in between. Then the psalmist directed his words to all of mankind: kings and commoners, old and young, men and women.

What would it look like for us to live in such a way as to express our continual praise to the Lord? We are told in Revelation that a day will come when every creature in heaven, on earth, and under the earth will praise Him (Revelation 5:13). But what if we chose to do it now? What if we continually honored Him with our attitudes and our actions? May we be quick to give the Lord praise for all He has done for us. He is so very worthy of our worship.

We give You all the glory and honor, Lord. May
our lips always be filled with Your praises.

4

My *hope* is built
on nothing less

Than *Jesus*' blood
and righteousness;

I dare not *trust* the
sweetest frame,

But *wholly* lean
on Jesus' name.

MY HOPE IS BUILT ON NOTHING LESS

E dward Mote, a trained cabinetmaker, knew what it meant for something to be built correctly and sturdily. A cabinet that was pretty to look at but not strong enough to hold anything would have been pointless indeed. The same could be said regarding the hope of a believer. If it's built upon the pretty things of the world—pleasures, possessions, and popularity—but can't withstand the hardships of life, it would be pointless as well.

After many years as a cabinetmaker, Mote became a pastor and preached the gospel for more than twenty-five years. I can only imagine that, as he penned this beloved hymn based on the parable found in Luke 6:46–49 about a man building a house, he drew upon his own experiences as a builder. He knew the dangers of building something without a firm foundation.

Most of us aren't cabinetmakers by profession, but we all can understand the repercussions of trusting in the wrong things. We've built our houses on sand, so to speak, and found them to be incredibly unstable in times of storm. May this hymn serve as a reminder that anything less than Jesus' blood, no matter how sweet, will never suffice. No matter what the world offers us as a means of support, we can only lean on Jesus' name.

Lord, You are all the support we need in this unstable world. Help us to build our lives on You.

5

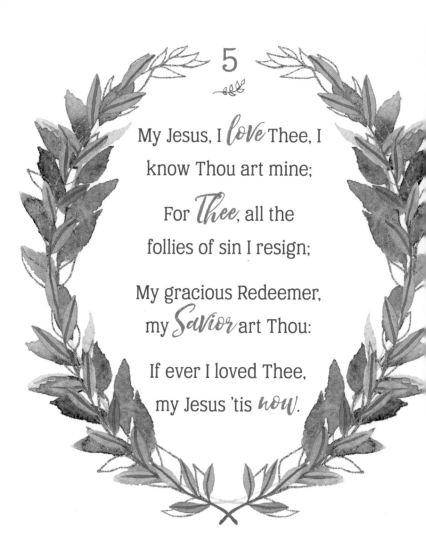

My Jesus, I *love* Thee, I know Thou art mine;

For *Thee*, all the follies of sin I resign;

My gracious Redeemer, my *Savior* art Thou:

If ever I loved Thee, my Jesus 'tis *now*.

MY JESUS, I LOVE THEE

Not much is known about William Ralph Featherston, the writer of this hymn. It is believed that he could have been as young as sixteen years old when he put these words to paper, that he died as a young man in his twenties, and that "My Jesus, I Love Thee" is the only song known to be written by him. Although Featherston may have been young in age, the theology in this hymn reveals a deep understanding of the gospel. Repentance, redemption, and relationship are all highlighted in this hymn. But beyond that, this was a love song from a sinner to a Savior.

It is reminiscent of another young man who wrote many songs now found in the book of Psalms. David sang often of his need for repentance, God as his Redeemer, and his relationship with the Lord. Yet there are also countless times when the sweet psalmist simply declared his love for the Lord. "I love the LORD, because He has heard my voice and my supplications" (Psalm 116:1).

In today's culture people claim to love everything from pop stars to pizza, but Featherston wrote of loving Jesus and described what that looked like for him. He experienced a personal relationship with Jesus, and that relationship gave him the desire to give up all the foolishness of sin. He knew Jesus intimately as Redeemer and Savior. When sixteen-year-old Featherston wrote "My Jesus, I Love Thee," it was the truest use of the word. May we love Jesus just as sincerely.

Thank You, Lord, for loving us and teaching
us how to love You in return.

6

O for a *thousand*
tongues to sing

My great
Redeemer's *praise*,

The *glories* of
my God and King,

The triumphs
of His *grace*.

O FOR A THOUSAND TONGUES TO SING

We don't always know what effect we have on those around us. Sometimes a simple act of kindness can make all the difference in somebody else's life. Bedridden with sickness, Charles Wesley was visited by some friends. They met some of his basic needs and shared with him what the Lord had been doing in their lives. At a time when Wesley's faith was faltering, these intentional acts of love were exactly what he needed.

One year after this bout of sickness, Wesley was inspired to write a hymn describing his faith and how it had been strengthened by those who cared for him. In that original writing, the seventh verse contains the words "O for a thousand tongues to sing." It was a paraphrase of a statement by Bishop Peter Bohler, who once said to Wesley, "If I had a thousand tongues, I would praise God with them all."

In Psalm 35, David described the evils that he was facing and included a request for God's intervention. In verse 28, he ended his long prayer with the certainty that, one day, his tongue would tell of the Lord's righteousness and would be filled with the Lord's praise all day long. True to his word, David penned many a psalm extolling his God. Like the bishop and Wesley, David would certainly have praised the Lord with a thousand tongues if he had had them.

Lord, You are worthy of my praise. May I never stop speaking of Your goodness and grace toward me.

7

More about Jesus
would I know,

More of His *grace*
to others show;

More of His
saving fullness see,

More of His *love*
who died for me.

MORE ABOUT JESUS

I would wager that it is during times of heartache and hardship that we draw the nearest and cling to Jesus. After all, some of the most moving portions of Scripture were written by individuals experiencing seasons of rejection, loneliness, and pain. Likewise, many of the hymns we love and cherish were penned by those going through tremendous losses and trials. So many stories of sorrow resulted in hymns of faith and praise to the One who strengthens the weak and weary.

Eliza Edmunds Hewitt wrote "More About Jesus" as she lay confined to her bed after a spinal injury. Once a schoolteacher with her whole life ahead of her, she found herself to be mostly an invalid. What was on her heart and mind as she spent so many hours unable to do the things she once did? What did she desire for herself? More of Jesus. More of His grace. More of His fullness. More of His love. Eliza had discovered what so many of us need to understand. Jesus is enough.

Paul preached this same message to the Colossian believers when he said, "You are complete in Him" (2:10). Christ is all we need, and He is more than enough to satisfy and sustain us. Jesus is enough whether we are traveling the world or confined to our beds. He is sufficient when our bank accounts are full and when we are overdrawn. Whatever our current circumstances, may the cries of our hearts always be for more of Jesus.

Lord, You are more than enough for me, and nothing this world has to offer can even come close.

8

Turn your *eyes*
upon Jesus,

Look full in His
wonderful face;

And the things of *earth*
will grow strangely dim

In the *light* of His
glory and grace.

TURN YOUR EYES UPON JESUS

Most of us desire to lead lives completely devoted to Jesus, yet we would also readily admit that we fall far short of that goal. The biggest issue for many of us is the abundance of distractions around us. Our eyes are constantly being drawn away from what matters and toward things that hold no eternal significance. We simply lose focus.

I went through a phase when I thought I wanted to learn how to play golf. I took a total of one lesson, so I was clearly not committed. But I still remember the first lesson to playing golf successfully: you must aim. Your eyes and your swing are directed where you want the ball to go. In other words, you must focus.

Helen Howarth Lemmel wrote "Turn Your Eyes upon Jesus" after reading a gospel tract written by a missionary. The theme of the tract was about one's focus, and, after reading it, Lemmel wrote the hymn that encouraged believers to focus on Jesus. Her words were reminiscent of those we read in Hebrews 12:2, which also instructs us to fix our eyes on Jesus.

We will follow whatever we have fixed our eyes upon. If we focus on riches, then we will pursue things that reward us financially. If we are fixated on pleasure, then we will seek to satisfy selfish desires. But if we turn our eyes on Jesus, we will find ourselves desiring the things that make us more like Him. And everything else will grow strangely dim.

> Father, please give me a laser-like focus so
> that everything I am is chasing after You.

9

Just as I am,

without one plea,

But that Thy blood

was *shed* for me,

And that *Thou* bid'st me

come to Thee,

O *Lamb* of God,

I come! I come!

JUST AS I AM

Have you ever wondered if you were enough? Maybe you felt inadequate for a task you were given or a situation that came your way. It could be that you have felt like a disappointment in some area of your life. These occasional moments of self-doubt are common across humanity, and they often come into play in a relationship with the Lord.

Charlotte Elliott wrote the words to one of the world's most famous hymns, "Just as I Am," during a moment of intense self-doubt. Her brother, a reverend, was planning an event to help underprivileged girls with their education. Elliott was plagued with feelings of uselessness and uncertainty as to how she could contribute. She became uncertain of her very salvation.

Elliott decided to write down everything she knew to be true of God, of herself, and of her relationship to Him. She told herself the gospel all over again and at the end of it was reminded that she was accepted by the Beloved just as she was. She realized that the state of her salvation was not based on her feelings but on the work of Jesus Christ.

It is the story of each and every believer. We come to Jesus feeling broken and helpless and undeserving of God's grace. We all come to Him the same—just as we are—and claiming the blood of Christ.

> Lord, there is nothing in me deserving of
> Your love. But I come to You just as I am.

10

What a *friend* we have
in Jesus, all our sins
and griefs to bear!

What a privilege to *carry*
everything to God in prayer!

O what *peace* we often forfeit,
O what needless pain we bear,

All because we do not carry
everything to God in prayer.

WHAT A FRIEND WE HAVE IN JESUS

I've experienced the loss of friendships due to distance, death, and divorce—none of which were pleasant. There is something in us that longs for a forever kind of friend. We yearn to be fully known and fully loved by someone who won't walk away when we need them most. This hymn has been the soundtrack of my life, playing softly in the background during my loneliest of times.

How appropriate that it was written by a son for his mother during a time when they were separated by a great distance and she was, undoubtedly, feeling alone. Joseph M. Scriven was a nineteenth-century pastor living in Canada. His mother, however, resided in Ireland. What a comfort it must have been to be reminded that she had a forever friend in Jesus Christ.

When speaking to His disciples, Jesus Himself said, "I have called you friends" (John 15:15). This was a significant shift in that the disciples were now privy to everything the Father told the Son. Jesus said that He had made all things known to them, and, through Scripture, He has made all things known to us as well. What a friend *we* have in Jesus still today. He is a friend like no other, and it's a friendship that nothing or no one can take from us. Jesus is a forever kind of friend.

What a friend we have in You, Lord. Thank You for the steadfastness and faithfulness of Your friendship.

11

I love to tell
the *story*,

'Twill be my
theme in glory

To *tell* the old,
old story

Of Jesus and
His *love*.

I LOVE TO TELL THE STORY

Katherine Hankey was an evangelist in the 1800s. She traveled and spent her days sharing the good news of the gospel. At one point, while in Africa, Hankey became seriously ill and spent a long time trying to recover. It was during this low point in her life that she wrote a very long poem on the life of Christ. The latter half of the poem became the hymn "I Love to Tell the Story."

Seriously ill and far from home, Hankey didn't write any "woe is me" words. Instead she proclaimed her love for sharing the gospel with others. She was still enthusiastic about telling people about the love of Jesus. The poem from which these lyrics were taken had fifty verses describing her love for Jesus and for sharing His story—fifty verses outlining the passion and purpose of our Savior. How long she must have pondered the person of Christ!

We often make ourselves the main character (sometimes even the hero) of our salvation stories. But it's always about Jesus. The psalmist declared in Psalm 66:16, "Come and hear, all you who fear God, and I will declare what He has done for my soul." Our testimonies are not about what we've done, be it good or bad, but about what Jesus has done on our behalf. He is the source of our healing and the hero of our story. Do we love to tell it?

Lord, may I never miss an opportunity
to tell the old, old story.

12

Take my *life*,
and let it be

Consecrated,

Lord, to Thee;

Take my moments,
and my *days*,

Let them *flow* in
ceaseless praise.

TAKE MY LIFE, AND LET IT BE

What would our lives look like if they were completely handed over to the Lord? Imagine every ounce of energy, every bit of ambition, and every speck of talent all committed to the things of God and His kingdom. What could the Lord do with a person so committed to Him? The possibilities are unlimited.

Frances Havergal's thoughts must have been running along those lines when she wrote the lyrics to "Take My Life, and Let It Be." In this hymn, she asked the Lord to take and use everything about her for His glory. Her hands, feet, voice, wealth, and intellect were all at His disposal. Frances offered all that she was for God to use as He saw fit.

Paul shared this same sentiment with the Philippians when he wrote, "For to me, to live is Christ" (1:21). For Paul, to be alive meant to use all that he was in service to Jesus. At times it was his voice used to share the gospel. Other times it was his very body being used for his devotion to Christ. For Paul, whatever the Lord needed to use to further His kingdom's purpose was His to use.

What would it look like for us to live such lives? Could we loosen our grip on the things of this world to which we cling? Do we trust God enough to put it all in His hands? Take our lives, and let them be consecrated, Lord, to Thee.

> Lord, You are worth giving our all. Use
> every part of us for Your glory.

13

I've got *peace*
like a river,

I've got peace
like a river,

I've got peace
like a *river*

in my *soul*.

I'VE GOT PEACE LIKE A RIVER

There is something calming about the sound of flowing water. Whether it's waves crashing against the shore, steady rain falling on a roof, or a recording of a babbling brook, most of us can easily grasp the connection between a lazy river and a peaceful feeling. But what about when the river is only in our imagination? Can we still have peace like a river when our situation is less than ideal?

Perhaps it would be interesting to learn that "I've Got Peace Like a River" is an African American spiritual. The words were not sung by those enjoying a day at the beach but by those laboring in fields while enduring the heat of the day. The people would sing to pass the time, to encourage one another, and to be reminded of a peace that was present—no matter the circumstances—even when those circumstances included slavery.

Peace is available to everyone in Christ. In Colossians 3:15, Paul instructed the people to let the peace of God rule in their hearts. We can have peace like a river no matter where we find ourselves when God is the provider of our peace. What would it look like for us to let that peace, as Paul described, rule in our hearts? It can have control over uncertainty and anxiety. Our peace can prevail over our problems. Wherever today finds you or whatever finds you today, you can have peace like a river in your soul.

Lord, You promise perfect peace to those whose minds
are fixed on You. Help me to do just that today.

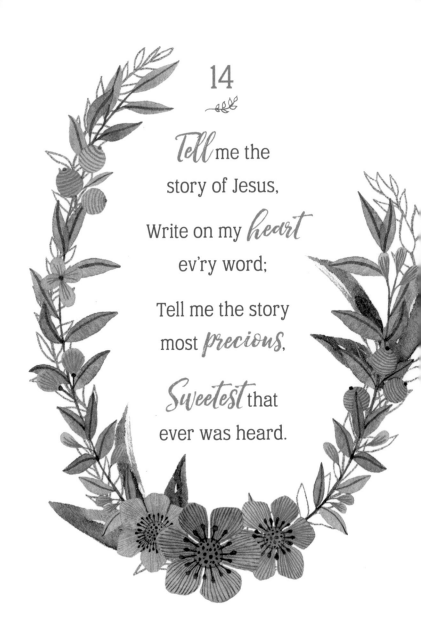

14

Tell me the
story of Jesus,

Write on my _heart_
ev'ry word;

Tell me the story
most _precious,_

Sweetest that
ever was heard.

TELL ME THE STORY OF JESUS

My children love to hear their grandparents tell stories. Their favorites, of course, usually involve their mom and dad as kids. Even though they've heard them before, they beg to hear all of the details time and time again. They never tire of hearing the stories, and Grandma and Grandpa never tire of telling them. A good story simply never grows old.

Fanny Crosby is the author behind some of the most beloved hymns of all time. It is said that she wrote over eight thousand during the course of her lifetime. Her story is one of tragedy and sorrow. Blinded at the age of six weeks by a mistreated eye infection, Crosby spent her life in physical darkness. Yet it is obvious by reading her words that she had an uncanny ability to see the Lord at work all around her. Perhaps it's because she didn't spend time wallowing in the potential self-pity of her own story but instead delighted in the story of Jesus.

"Tell me the story of Jesus." What a story it is! The Son of God was wrapped in flesh and sent into the world. He lived a life of labor and love, and then suffered and died on behalf of sinners. He entered the grave, defeated death, and rose victorious over the enemy. And now Jesus reigns in heaven while we eagerly await His return. It is, as Crosby penned, a story most precious. It's a story that never grows old.

Lord, I never tire of hearing the
story of Your love for me.

15

There is a *balm* in Gilead

To make the wounded whole;

There is a balm in *Gilead*

To *heal* the sin-sick soul.

THERE IS A BALM IN GILEAD

In Old Testament times there was a region near the Jordan River known for a certain type of tree. People would make the journey to the area for healing of various kinds. Physicians would make a balm from the gum of the tree that was believed to be a miracle cure. The region was called Gilead. Through the prophet Jeremiah, God told the people that the balm of Gilead would never cure what really ailed them. He told the people that the healing they truly needed could not be accomplished with earthly, man-made medicines.

Although the phrase "balm in Gilead" appears in the Old Testament (Jeremiah 8:22), this African American spiritual refers to another, less literal type of balm. The lyrics speak to a New Testament healing found only in Jesus. It describes the very healing people have always needed. It's a healing that we will not experience this side of heaven.

Every person who has ever walked the earth has experienced the kind of wounding and soul sickness described in "There Is a Balm in Gilead." There are areas of hurt that can't be addressed with earthly measures. There are sins with which our flesh will continually struggle. There is a healing that can happen only when we are in the presence of Jesus, the balm of heaven.

Lord, I long for the day I experience the
healing found in Your presence.

16

Jesus, Jesus,
Jesus,

Sweetest name
I know,

Fills my ev'ry
longing,

Keeps me
singing as I go.

HE KEEPS ME SINGING

In Psalm 40:3, David wrote that God had put a new song in his mouth. By itself that verse sounds nice and would look lovely printed on a coffee mug, but the power of that verse is found in the ones that precede it. David described himself as crying from the bottom of a "horrible pit." The beauty of this new song he had been given was found in the fact that he was able to sing it after enduring so much.

When Luther Bridgers wrote "He Keeps Me Singing," he had no way of knowing what he would eventually experience. Only a year after his song first appeared in a hymnal in 1910, Bridgers's wife and children died in a house fire. Following this great tragedy, he continued to preach revivals across the South. He kept proclaiming the goodness of God and the gospel. It was certainly only Jesus who could have kept him singing after such heartache.

What we learn from the testimonies of people like David and Bridgers is that our circumstances don't have to steal our song. We may cry out from the bottom of a horrible pit. Or experience a heart-crushing loss. Or feel the sting of disappointment. But God, in a way only He can do, can place a new song in our hearts. He can keep us going and keep us singing as we go. And the beauty of the song will be that we continue to sing it no matter what comes our way.

Lord, help me to keep singing Your praises
no matter what comes my way.

17

Immortal, invisible,
God only *wise*,
In *light* inaccessible
hid from our eyes,

Most blessed, most
glorious, the
Ancient of Days,
Almighty, victorious,
Thy great name we praise.

IMMORTAL, INVISIBLE, GOD ONLY WISE

There are some songs that we sing because they make us feel uplifted. Other songs bring about a reverence for the sacrifice of Christ. Still others give us hope by describing the beauty and blessings that await us in heaven. This hymn is in a class by itself in that it describes the deep and unchanging attributes of God.

One could do a deep theological study based only on the words of this hymn written by Walter Chalmers Smith. The opening line alone references the immortality and omniscience of the Father. It goes on to speak of the all-powerful, steadfast nature of God. It is reminiscent of Paul's words to Timothy: "Now to the King eternal, immortal, invisible, to God who alone is wise, be honor and glory forever and ever. Amen" (1 Timothy 1:17).

When we have walked with God for a long time, we sometimes lose sight of His holiness and power. We approach Him in a casual manner or fail to recognize the wonder that we can approach Him at all. If we read and meditate on the lyrics of Smith's hymn, we are reminded that God is almighty and glorious. He is filled with wisdom and justice. He is worthy of glory and honor and praise. And because of the blood of Jesus, we have access to Him. Hallelujah!

Thank You, Lord, for making a way for us
to have a relationship with a holy God.

18

O Beulah Land,

Sweet

Beulah Land!

As on thy

highest

Mount

I stand.

BEULAH LAND

When we become Christ-followers, we also become, by default, exiles on earth. As such, we often find ourselves weary of this world and incredibly homesick for heaven. How could we not be when we know what awaits us? No matter what temporary comforts we accumulate for ourselves, the fact remains that this is not our eternal home.

Written by Edgar Page Stites and composed by John R. Sweney, "Beulah Land" is a hymn derived from Isaiah 24: "Thou shalt no more be termed Forsaken; neither shall thy land any more be termed Desolate; but thou shalt be called Hephzibah and thy land Beulah; for the LORD delighteth in thee, and thy land shall be married" (KJV).

The prophet Isaiah spoke of a time when the Hebrews would return to God and no longer experience exile in Babylon. He saw a day when their land would no longer be desolate but would be renamed Beulah, which means *married* in Hebrew (Isaiah 62:4). How they must have looked forward to that day. How they must have longed for Beulah Land.

All who are in Christ anxiously await our heavenly home. We eagerly anticipate a place without sickness, heartache, or loss. Most of all, we look forward to a time when we see Jesus face to face. Although separated by more than a hundred years, we share with Stites and Sweney the deep longing for sweet Beulah Land.

Lord, may we never grow too comfortable here but always be homesick for heaven until we stand in Your presence.

19

Rescue the
perishing,
Care for
the dying;

Jesus is
merciful,
Jesus
will save.

RESCUE THE PERISHING

Fanny Crosby wrote "Rescue the Perishing" in 1869 after visiting a New York City mission, meeting the men who lived there, and being concerned about their well-being. That night, after returning home, Crosby penned these words that would offer comfort to countless people throughout the following century.

We are surrounded daily by people who are suffering, struggling, and seeking. In his book of wisdom, Solomon said that we should not expect to stand before the Lord and claim ignorance regarding the countless needs around us (Proverbs 24:12).

Scripture is clear that we are to take action. We are instructed to rescue those who, through injustice or neglect, are suffering. We are to hold back those who are stumbling down the road to destruction. Over and over in God's Word are commands to do good.

We must care enough to take action. If any person crosses our path and doesn't come to saving faith, may it not be because we didn't plead with them to join us in heaven. As Charles Spurgeon said, "If sinners be damned, at least let them leap to hell over our dead bodies. And if they perish, let them perish with our arms wrapped about their knees. If hell must be filled, let it be filled in the teeth of our exertions, and let not one go unwarned and unprayed for."

Make it be our heart's cry, Lord, that
the perishing would be rescued.

20

Count

your blessings,

name them

one by one;

Count your

many *blessings*,

see what

God hath done.

COUNT YOUR BLESSINGS

One of more than three thousand hymns written by Johnson Oatman Jr., "Count Your Blessings" is a reminder to practice being grateful. A preacher once described a scene of a place in heaven that held all of the unopened gifts of believers. It was an image of the many things available and not yet accessed by Christ followers on earth. The story was fictitious yet held a kernel of truth.

We tend to live at such a fast pace that we miss out on many of the gifts that God intended for us to enjoy. Think about all of the things that God did purely for our pleasure: the elegant neck of a giraffe, the vibrant colors of a sunset, the peaceful sound of the wind rustling through the leaves. We allow so many things to slip by unnoticed.

What would life be like if we chose to go to all the places? Let's make it our goal to see all the things. Listen to all the music. Read all the books. Meet all the people. Make as many friends as we can. Tell all the jokes. Forgive all the offenses. Drink all the coffee. Enjoy all the breezes. Savor all the sunsets. We don't want to leave unopened a single good and perfect gift (James 1:17) from our Creator.

One way to be intentional about practicing gratitude, as the old hymn says, is to count your many blessings. Take time to record the many ways God lavishes His love upon you, then name them one by one to ensure you enjoy every single gift.

Father, open our eyes to the good and
perfect gifts all around us.

21

From all that *dwell*
below the skies,

Let the Creator's praise arise;

Let the Redeemer's
name be sung

Through ev'ry *land*
by ev'ry tongue.

FROM ALL THAT DWELL BELOW THE SKIES

When Isaac Watts wrote that every land and every tongue should sing the praises of the Lord, he couldn't have known how far the gospel would spread. He couldn't have imagined that some of the largest gatherings would be found in Brazil and South Korea. He probably never imagined the magnitude and multitude of "all that dwell below the skies." The same could probably be said of the psalmist when he declared, "Laud Him, all you peoples" (Psalm 117:1). How could they have known that the gospel would spread like wildfire? That people would lay down their lives for it? That the church would grow far beyond their imaginations?

Do you know who *could* imagine it though? John could because he had been given a glimpse of how every tribe and tongue would look. He described it this way: "After these things I looked, and behold, a great multitude which no one could number, of all nations, tribes, peoples, and tongues, standing before the throne and before the Lamb, clothed with white robes, with palm branches in their hands" (Revelation 7:9).

One day, all who have placed their faith and hope in the sacrifice Jesus made on the cross will experience it for themselves. We all will worship God with those who have dwelt below the skies. What a day that will be.

Lord, I can't wait to be among the throng
gathered around Your throne.

22

Are you *washed*
in the blood,

In the soul-cleansing
blood of the *Lamb*?

Are your *garments* spotless?
Are they white as snow?

Are *you* washed in the
blood of the Lamb?

ARE YOU WASHED IN THE BLOOD?

What does it mean to be a Christ follower? How do you explain the gospel to someone who isn't familiar with it? Written in 1878, this hymn is one of many written by Elisha Hoffman. In four stanzas, Hoffman offers some deep biblical truths by presenting several questions one could ask himself regarding his relationship with Jesus.

The first line of the song tells the listener where he can turn to be cleansed of his sins. In those opening questions, Hoffman first makes it clear that Jesus is the source of cleansing and that it is all an act of grace. The second verse speaks to the daily devotion necessary. Repentance is addressed in the final lines. He presents the entire gospel in one beautiful song. Along with the rich theology is the beautiful imagery of believers wearing their robes of white.

The idea of a crowd of people wearing white robes is pulled from Revelation 7:13–14. Seeing the crowd around the throne, John asked the identity of the group. The elder told him, "These are the ones who come out of the great tribulation, and washed their robes and made them white in the blood of the Lamb."

The next time you have an opportunity to share the truth of the gospel with someone, simply think through the questions asked in this hymn. They will certainly open the door to a conversation regarding the cleansing power of the blood of Christ.

Thank You, Lord, for Your soul-cleansing blood.

23

This is my
Father's *world*,

And to *my*
list'ning ears

All *nature* sings,
and round me rings

The music of
the *spheres*.

THIS IS MY FATHER'S WORLD

What is your favorite part of God's creation? Are you in awe of the ocean, or are you at home in the mountains? Perhaps you're a bird watcher, a storm chaser, or a stargazer. Is it the sound of the wind, the sight of a sunset, or the smell of lilac that makes you catch your breath? Maybe you've been mesmerized by a spider's web or enjoyed the shade of an old oak tree.

Reverend Babcock lived in New York and would often take walks outdoors to enjoy nature. He would tell his wife that he was going out to "see the Father's world." Following Babcock's death, his wife published some of his writings, which included a poem entitled "My Father's World." Babcock knew whose world it was that he was enjoying.

The creation account described in Genesis is most likely familiar. But if we aren't careful, we will read the words and miss the wonder. God designed and created a world that was perfect for the crème de la crème of His creative efforts: you and me. The thick mane of a lion and the delicate wings of a butterfly, shooting stars and crashing waves, cool breezes on hot summer days, the smell of rain and the colors of a rainbow—this is our Father's world, and His fingerprints are all over it.

Thank You, Father, for the beauty of Your creation.
I am in awe of the nature that surrounds me.

24

Who is *he* in
yonder stall,

At whose feet the
shepherds fall?

Who is he in
deep distress,

Fasting in the
wilderness?

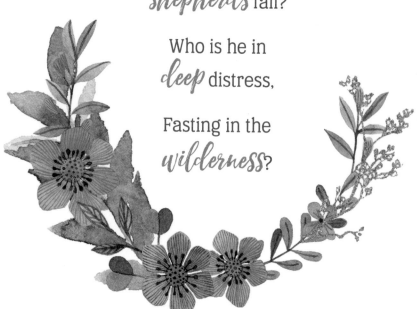

WHO IS HE IN YONDER STALL

Benjamin Russell Hanby accomplished many things in his short thirty-three years. He opened a singing school and worked as a teacher, a minister, and an editor. No doubt he did many other things that were simply not recorded. Among all of his other dealings, he also found time to point others to Christ by writing more than five hundred songs before he died. One of those hymns, "Who Is He in Yonder Stall," quickly takes the listener through the life of Christ.

From Jesus' humble birth in a manger, to His earthly ministry of teaching and healing, to His death on the tree, and finishing with His victory over death, Hanby told the whole story in song. Then he made it clear that the song wasn't about any ordinary man. Oh, no. The question posed was, "Who is He?" And the answer, time and again, was, "'Tis the Lord, 'Tis the Lord." Hanby then made it clear that the only acceptable response to such a revelation was to fall at Jesus' feet and "crown Him, crown Him, Lord of all!"

Although it's been over 150 years since this hymn was written, the question posed is just as real and relevant today. *Who is He?* The answer is so vital that Jesus Himself posed the question to His disciples. "He said to them, 'But who do you say that I am?'" (Luke 9:20). Peter, often the spokesperson for the group, emphatically declared, "The Christ of God." The only question that remains is: who is He to you?

Lord, You are the Christ of God, the Lord of all.

25

So I'll *cherish* the

old rugged cross,

Till my trophies at
last I lay down;

I will *cling* to the

old rugged cross,

And exchange it

some day for a *crown*.

THE OLD RUGGED CROSS

George Bennard was born in Youngstown, Ohio, in 1873, less than forty-five minutes from my own hometown of Alliance. He also happened to be the writer of one of my all-time favorite hymns, "The Old Rugged Cross." It is arguably the most beloved hymn of all time.

After coming to Christ during a Salvation Army meeting, Bennard and his wife became active in the Methodist Church. It is said that he wrote "The Old Rugged Cross" in response to some ridicule he had received. The source or topic of the ridicule isn't clear, but his response is found in the lyrics of the hymn. His answer was to cling to the cross. He is reported to have said that, for him, "Christ and the cross were inseparable."

Perhaps it is best that we do not know the specific reason Bennard was ridiculed. Who among us has not faced criticism or torment of some kind? We can relate to his situation without knowing the details—maybe even more so because we do not know the details. We can then apply his answer to anything we encounter. The answer is always to cling to the cross.

Have you ever been mocked for your faith? Cling to the cross. Have you ever been misunderstood? Cling to the cross. Have you endured hardship and heartache? Cling, sweet friend, to the cross. Don't be afraid to bear its shame and reproach because, one day, you'll exchange it for a crown.

Lord, help me to always be true to the cross.

26

There is a *fountain*
filled with blood

Drawn from

Immanuel's veins;

And sinners, *plunged*

beneath that flood,

Lose *all* their

guilty stains.

THERE IS A FOUNTAIN

Our deepest praise is often a result of our darkest days. "There Is a Fountain" was written by William Cowper after he endured his first major bout of depression. His chronic depression would be a thorn in the flesh his entire life. He would attempt suicide at one point, be hospitalized, and experience a short period of stability. But depression would eventually rear its ugly head again and become the voice behind many of his hymns. So his songs certainly held a serious tone, overflowing with biblical truth and comfort.

I can't help but imagine God Himself reaching through the darkness of Cowper's depression and speaking truth to his soul. Then those sweet truths would flow through him and come out in song. Not even the darkness of depression could separate Cowper from the love of God.

We all go through periods of darkness in our lives. Perhaps some of them are shorter than others. There are certainly many of us intimately acquainted with depression and all that it entails. So many people live at war with their own minds, and it is often greatly misunderstood by the people around them. But God knows how to speak to His children. There is not a single day when any of us are unseen or forgotten. Healing and hope are still—always—available. There is still a fountain filled with blood (Zechariah 13:1) that we can come to time and time again.

Thank You, Lord, for Your precious blood
that still cleanses and heals today.

27

And He *walks* with me,
and He talks with me,

And He tells me I am His *own*,

And the *joy* we share
as we tarry there,

None other has *ever* known.

IN THE GARDEN

Where do you go when you want to have time alone with God? Perhaps you go to your favorite chair with a cozy blanket and your Bible. Maybe you sit on your porch with a view of rolling hills, an oceanfront, or some other beautiful scenery. It could be that you, like this hymn described, spend time walking in the garden with the Lord. Then again, it's possible that your life is complicated and chaotic and there isn't a perfect and peaceful place for you to slip away to be alone with your Savior. The latter scenario is the case for many of us, which is what makes the story behind "In the Garden" so wonderful.

When C. Austin Miles penned this hymn, he was not in the habit of walking in the garden. In fact, according to his great-granddaughter, it was written in a dark, dreary, and leaky basement in New Jersey. Not only did he not have a view of a garden, he didn't even have a window. Yet, in his mind's eye, he saw a garden perfectly and wrote in such a way as to make all who read and sing his words feel that they were walking right along beside him.

"In the Garden" is a beautiful reminder that we can be alone with God regardless of our circumstances. Whether we are walking in a garden in the early morning hours or sitting in a cold basement in the middle of winter, Scripture reminds us that God is always in our midst (Zephaniah 3:17).

> I'm so grateful, Lord, that wherever I am, You still walk with me and talk with me.

28

Softly and tenderly
Jesus is calling,

Calling for *you*
and for me;

See, on the portals He's
waiting and watching,

Watching for
you and for me!

SOFTLY AND TENDERLY

All throughout Scripture we see instances of Jesus being moved with compassion. Nowhere are His words more tender than in His invitation for us to come and find rest in Him. "Come to Me," the Savior calls to all who are weary and burdened (Matthew 11:28). Who among us, at a low point in our lives, wouldn't love to hear the gentle voice of Jesus calling us to His side?

Perhaps that is why "Softly and Tenderly" is the most widely known and circulated of Will Thompson's compositions. Famed evangelist Dwight L. Moody was taken with the hymn and its writer. Once, during a time of illness and isolation, Moody insisted on seeing Thompson. He shared with Thompson that he would rather have written "Softly and Tenderly" than anything he had accomplished in his own life.

There is certainly something irresistible in the way our Savior woos us. Wherever we have roamed and however far we have strayed, Jesus still calls softly and tenderly to His children, inviting them to come home.

Lord, thank You for Your love and compassion toward us that compels You to call us home.

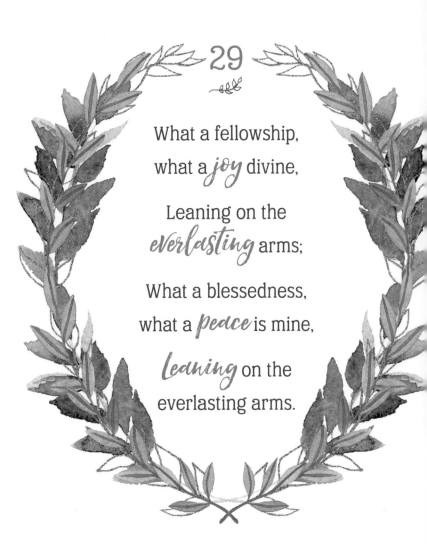

29

What a fellowship,
what a *joy* divine,

Leaning on the
everlasting arms;

What a blessedness,
what a *peace* is mine,

Leaning on the
everlasting arms.

LEANING ON THE EVERLASTING ARMS

Where do you turn when life is discouraging, disappointing, or downright devastating? The answer to that question must be decided before the hardships happen. We need to know, on the front end, where we will go when things go awry. The world will certainly offer us several options, and, in a moment of pain, any of them may seem reasonable. But the comfort we need during times of tremendous loss can't be found in any person, possession, or pleasure.

Anthony J. Showalter and Elisha Hoffman knew where true peace and comfort were found. In 1887 Showalter received a letter from not one but two of his former pupils informing him that their wives had died. Upon hearing of their devastating loss, he thought of Deuteronomy 33:27: "The eternal God is your refuge, and underneath are the everlasting arms." In response to the letters from his pupils, he was reminded of where true comfort comes from.

Joy and peace are available to us when we choose to lean on the everlasting arms of God. It is a joy and peace that can't be shaken or taken by any circumstances we encounter. There isn't an earthly substitute. The everlasting arms never lose their power or fail to support us when we lean on them.

What a beautiful reminder that, when we walk with God, we are held in His unshakeable grip. No one can remove us from His hands. He is our strong tower and our refuge. What a joy it is to lean on His everlasting arms.

Lord, we are forever supported by Your everlasting
arms. May we lean on You whatever comes our way.

30

Rock of Ages, cleft for me,

Let me hide myself in Thee;

Let the *water* and the blood,

From Thy wounded
side which flowed,

Be of sin the
double cure,

Save from wrath and
make me *pure*.

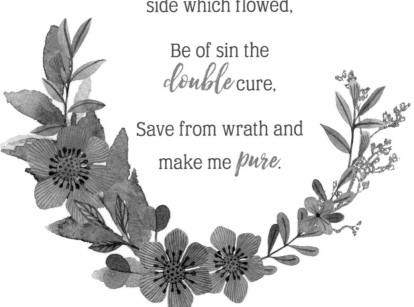

ROCK OF AGES

Where do you run when life becomes difficult? Where do you seek shelter from the storms that rage? Whether we're struggling with financial distress, relationship issues, or health battles, we all experience moments when we simply want to hide. We long to be tucked away safely somewhere.

The idea behind the hymn "Rock of Ages" came to Reverend Augustus Toplady when he was caught in a storm while traveling along a gorge in England in 1763. As he hid in a crevice of the rock to protect himself from the raging storm, the title and initial lyrics came to him. The words of his song give us such a vivid mental image of what David must have had in mind when he referred to God as his rock of refuge (Psalm 94:22). David, too, had spent some time hiding in the clefts of rocks. Although he was often hiding from his enemies, the safety he found was the same.

As followers of Christ, we can find protection in the presence of the Rock of Ages. Just like Toplady and David hid in the cleft of an actual rock, we can run to God, our Rock of Refuge, and find shelter from the storms of life. He will, as the hymn says, allow us to hide ourselves in Him.

This hymn speaks to our greatest protection of all. We are hidden from the wrath of God. Covered in the blood of Christ, we are made pure and saved from the penalty of sin. It is called the *double cure*. Whatever you are encountering today, you can run to the Rock of Ages.

Lord, You are my source of safety and
security. I will always run to You.

31

When peace like a
river, attendeth my way,

When sorrows like
sea *billows* roll;

Whatever my lot, Thou
hast taught me to say,

"It is *well*, it is well
with my soul."

IT IS WELL WITH MY SOUL

Horatio Spafford's story has been told countless times over the years. There may not be another person who has suffered such tremendous loss and responded in such a way. He did, at one point, have it all in terms of what the world would call success. He was a successful businessman with a nice family. But in a story reminiscent of Job's, it was all taken away from him.

Spafford buried his two-year-old son and then lost all of his financial resources in the Great Chicago Fire of 1871. In an attempt to have a fresh start, the family decided to go to Europe. Spafford sent his wife and daughters on ahead of him, and, sadly, their ship sank. He received a message from his wife that simply said, "Saved alone." He had lost all four of his daughters.

While passing over the waters where he had lost his daughters, the words of this hymn came to him. "It is well, it is well with my soul." What did he mean that it was well with his soul? That in times of peace and in times of sorrow his response would be the same. Although Spafford had lost everything this earth calls good, he still could say, "It is well with my soul" because he had experienced the peace that surpasses all understanding (Philippians 4:7) that is promised to us as believers. When we know Christ as our Lord and Savior, we, too, can say that no matter the circumstances, "It is well with my soul."

Lord, thank You for the ever-present
peace of Your presence.

32

Jesus *loves* me,
this I know,
For the *Bible*
tells me so.
Little ones
to Him belong;

They are weak,
but *He* is strong.

JESUS LOVES ME

Written by Anna Bartlett Warner, "Jesus Loves Me," contains one of the greatest truths of Scripture. Often thought of as a children's song, it is a concept with which some of the most mature Christians struggle. The idea that Jesus could love us so much that He gave His life, for us, is mind-boggling. Yet when understood and internalized, it has the power to change everything.

Jesus openly declared His love for His disciples. In John 13:34, He instructed them to love each other as He loved them. Jesus went on to describe His love for them as being the same as the Father's love for Him (John 15:9). We can't even fathom the love the Father has for the Son! Then Jesus proved His love for us by laying down His life on our behalf, which He described as the greatest love of all (John 15:13). Jesus loves us.

How did Warner know that Jesus loved her? Did she hear an audible voice? Was it spelled out in the clouds? There is something beautiful in the knowledge that she learned of His love the same way we learn of it. It's the same way every person, young or old, can know that Jesus loves them—because the Bible tells us so.

The Bible is one long love letter from God to His children. We have the luxury, at any point in time, to open up the pages of Scripture and remind ourselves that Jesus loves us. We can know it's true because the Bible tells us so.

*Lord, to know that I am loved by You is
the most precious truth of all.*

33

'Tis so *sweet* to trust in Jesus,

Just to take Him at His *word*;

Just to *rest* upon His promise,

Just to *know*,

"Thus saith the Lord."

'TIS SO SWEET TO TRUST IN JESUS

Louisa Stead knew what it meant to trust in Jesus. When she wrote the lyrics to "'Tis So Sweet to Trust in Jesus" in 1882, she was a young widow who had long experienced poor health and was living as a missionary in South Africa. Stead trusted the Lord with her health, her life without her husband, and her future in a foreign country. In the face of all the unknowns in her life, she chose to take Jesus at His word and to rest upon His promises.

While you may not be a widow or a missionary overseas, there are probably situations in your life that are uncertain or scary. We all face an unknown future and must decide if we will choose faith or fear. Isaiah 12:2 is thought to be the inspiration for Stead's song and can serve as an anthem for every believer: "Behold, God is my salvation, I will trust and not be afraid."

What do you need to trust Jesus with today? Whatever it may be, your God can handle it. God has proven over and over that He is a keeper of His word. He fulfills every promise. He never leaves or forsakes His people. In a world where people are fickle, our God is faithful. And that is why it is so sweet to trust in Jesus.

Lord, it is so very sweet to trust in You. You
are my God, and I will not be afraid.

34

Showers of blessing,

Showers of *blessing* we need;

Mercy-drops, round us are *falling*,

But for the showers we *plead*.

THERE SHALL BE SHOWERS OF BLESSING

E zekiel 34:26–27 offers this beautiful picture of God lavishing His blessings on His people. "There shall be showers of blessing," God promised. The people would experience prosperity and protection. They would no longer live in fear of their enemies. They would be at peace with their God.

This is the passage Daniel W. Whittle was meditating on when he wrote this hymn in 1883. It pleads unashamedly for the promised blessings from the hand of the Lord. The lyrics cry out for refreshments and revival for God's people. Scripture tells us that sometimes we have not because we ask not. We have the privilege of coming boldly to the throne of grace and requesting anything of the Lord.

We often struggle because we expect far too little from the Lord. We often fail to ask Him to provide the things that He has promised to provide. We settle for the mercy drops, as Whittle described them in his hymn, but we fail to plead for the showers. Do you ever find yourself being content with a sprinkle when you have been promised so much more by your heavenly Father? Don't be timid in your requests. God longs to be gracious to you and shower you with His blessings.

Lord, You are a good, good God.
Shower us with Your blessings.

35

Stand up, *stand* up for Jesus,

Ye *soldiers* of the cross;

Lift high His *royal* banner,

It must not suffer loss.

STAND UP, STAND UP FOR JESUS

What would it look like for you to stand up for Jesus in the places where you live, work, and play? Have you ever felt compelled to speak out against injustice in some area of your life? There are numerous commands in Scripture to speak up for the needy and oppressed. As Christ followers, we live our lives under the royal banner of Jesus, and our allegiance is always and only to Him.

"Stand Up, Stand Up for Jesus" was written by George Duffield Jr., but it was based on the dying words of his associate, Dudley Atkins Tyng. Tyng was removed from his local Presbyterian community because of his outspoken views against slavery. Shortly following his removal, he was critically wounded in a farming accident. In one of his final conversations with his father, Tyng insisted that his brethren in the ministry everywhere be encouraged to stand up for Jesus.

Duffield gave the sermon at the memorial service for his friend, which he based on Ephesians 6:14: "Stand therefore, having girded your waist with truth, having put on the breastplate of righteousness." Following his message, Duffield closed by reciting the hymn he had written in honor of Tyng. Even after suffering rejection from his faith family, Tyng still encouraged other believers to stand up, stand up for Jesus. This brings us back to our original question. What would it look like for us to stand up for Jesus in our daily lives? And more importantly, are we willing to do it?

Lord, give me a boldness and courage to stand up
and be known as a disciple of Jesus Christ.

36

Onward,
Christian soldiers,

marching
as to war,

With the *cross*
of Jesus

going on
before!

ONWARD, CHRISTIAN SOLDIERS

I don't know about you, but I regret many of the things that I have said or done in haste. I often look back and think, *If only I had paused for a moment and given some thought to that.* But for Sabine Baring-Gould, the hastily written lyrics of "Onward, Christian Soldiers" have been blessing listeners for more than a century. He would often apologize for the fact that he had written it in such haste and that some of the lines may not be perfect. Obviously, no apologies were necessary. His hymn has been used by multiple organizations and entities over the years.

Baring-Gould based his song on 2 Timothy 2:3, which teaches, "You therefore must endure hardship as a good soldier of Jesus Christ." Both the hymn and Paul's words to Timothy liken the life of the believer to a soldier marching into battle. Paul described the focus and devotion required of a soldier, while Baring-Gould described the courage, boldness, and certain victory. Together they create a perfect picture of the life of a Christ follower.

Every day we have a battle raging around us and an enemy seeking to destroy us. Paul told Timothy that he must endure hardship as a good soldier. This meant that he could not abandon the mission. He could not change his mind when things become difficult. He had to carry on like a good soldier would. Baring-Gould's message was the same: "On then, Christian soldiers, on to victory."

Lord, give us the courage to follow You into
battle like brave soldiers of the cross.

37

When the trumpet of
the Lord shall *sound*,

and *time* shall be no more,

And the *morning* breaks,
eternal, bright, and fair;

When the saved of earth shall gather

over on the other *shore*,

And the *roll* is called up

yonder, I'll be there.

WHEN THE ROLL IS CALLED UP YONDER

James Milton Black was inspired to write this hymn after a literal calling of the roll in a Sunday school class he was teaching. A child was not there on a certain Sunday, and he felt compelled to go visit. It turned out that the child was suffering from pneumonia and needed a doctor's care. Between this situation and some time spent pondering the Book of Life mentioned in the Bible, Black was suddenly concerned over somebody not being present at the calling of the roll in heaven. It bothered him so much that he wrote this hymn.

There will be a day when the names of those in Christ will be called (Philippians 4:3). Are there individuals in our lives that may not be present when the roll is called in heaven? Most likely there are people all around us who are going about their lives unaware that they are on their way to eternal separation from God. We should desire that everyone we encounter be with us on that glorious day when we all gather on the other shore.

We should pray that God would give us eyes to see the lost and wandering people around us, as well as hearts that break for the souls of those we encounter every day as we go about our lives. There will certainly be those who are not present when the roll is called, but let it not be because they crossed our paths and were not told about Jesus.

Lord, I long for the day when I hear my name
and I see Your face. I will be there.

38

There's a land that
is fairer than *day*,

And by *faith*
we can see it afar;

For the Father
waits over the way

To prepare us a
dwelling place there.

THERE'S A LAND THAT IS FAIRER THAN DAY

The prophet Isaiah told of a place without sickness or sin (Isaiah 33:24). Don't we all long for such a place? We long for a home where our bodies don't wear out and loved ones don't walk out. Isn't it wonderful to know that the place described in Sanford Fillmore Bennett's hymn "There's a Land That Is Fairer Than Day" wasn't a figment of his imagination? There really is a dwelling place for us in heaven!

The home that awaits us is without sorrow and sighing. It will be filled with the sounds of singing and praise. But the very best part is that God the Father awaits us there. We will one day enjoy fellowship with our Creator as they once experienced in the garden. It's difficult to imagine such intimacy.

When Jesus knew His time had come to be crucified and resurrected, He warned the disciples. There were questions and confusion. The men just couldn't understand what He was telling them. Jesus' response is one of the sweetest promises in all of Scripture: "In My Father's house are many mansions; if it were not so, I would have told you. I go to prepare a place for you. And if I go and prepare a place for you, I will come again and receive you to Myself; that where I am, there you may be also" (John 14:2–3).

There is a land that is fairer than day. Jesus has gone to prepare it and has promised to return for us. See you there.

> Lord, I can't wait to stand on the shore of that
> place and bask in the light of Your presence.

39

On Jordan's stormy
banks I stand,

And cast a *wishful* eye

To Canaan's fair
and *happy* land,

Where my *possessions* lie.

ON JORDAN'S STORMY BANKS I STAND

Although it has been altered over the years, Samuel Stennett originally wrote "On Jordan's Stormy Banks I Stand" as if from the perspective of a believer approaching death. It's the story of someone who knows he is about to enter the heaven described in Revelation 22. It's a land without sorrow, sickness, or night. God reigns, and His glory lights the whole land. It is, as Stennett stated, a fair and happy land.

We've all heard stories of people on their deathbeds seeing visions or having various unusual experiences. I know nothing of the veracity of such accounts. God is certainly able to do far more than we can even imagine. What I do know to be true is that John was given a glimpse into glory and his description was breathtaking. I also know that Paul said that his desire concerning his life was to depart and be with Christ, which was far better (Philippians 1:23). "Better than what?" you ask. Better than anything else. Jesus said that He was preparing the place Himself!

For those who believe in Christ, the grave has no power, and death holds no fear. One day, we will all stand on Jordan's stormy banks and make the journey to our heavenly home. We know where we are going, and it is, as Stennett described, "that happy place." We will experience the peace and presence of the Father forever.

Lord, I long for the day when I experience
the home You have prepared for me.

40

I stand amazed
in the presence

Of Jesus
the Nazarene,

And *wonder* how
He could *love* me,

A sinner,
condemned, unclean.

I STAND AMAZED IN THE PRESENCE

Which famous person would you love to meet? Or which person, when you were in his or her presence, had you starstruck? For me, it was the time I saw William Lee Golden buying paper towels at the local grocery store. That may not mean much to some, but I'm a trucker's daughter, and he's an Oak Ridge Boy. In my world, it was a big deal. But no singer or movie star, no matter how famous or connected to our childhood, could compare to being in the presence of Jesus.

Hymn writer Charles H. Gabriel was rightly amazed at the magnitude of Jesus' love and sacrifice, perhaps because he had such an accurate view of himself. It's easy to convince ourselves that we aren't that bad—that we are good—but Jesus is better. The reality is that we, apart from Christ, are as Gabriel described: sinners, condemned, unclean. Only by being honest about our own state can we truly appreciate what Jesus did for us.

Jesus' love for us is the most genuine love of all. It is based on His goodness and not our own. Those drops of blood He sweat (Luke 22:41–44) were, as Gabriel wrote, for our griefs and not His own. He died for us while we were still enemies. "Amazed" will surely be an understatement of what we will feel in Christ's presence.

Lord, Thank You for Your love for me.
It will never cease to amaze me.

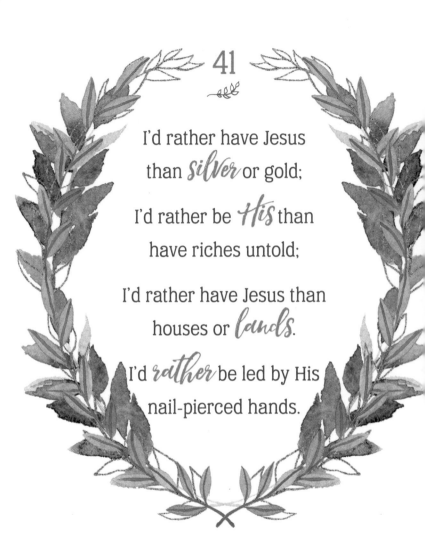

41

I'd rather have Jesus than *silver* or gold;

I'd rather be *His* than have riches untold;

I'd rather have Jesus than houses or *lands.*

I'd *rather* be led by His nail-pierced hands.

I'D RATHER HAVE JESUS

R hea Miller grew up with an alcoholic father and a mother who never stopped believing that God could change him. Many people prayed for Martin, and, eventually, he did give up alcohol. Rhea's dad not only placed his faith in Christ but also became a Baptist minister. Later in life, she wrote "I'd Rather Have Jesus" after hearing Martin declare that he would rather have Jesus than worldly riches.

The lyrics express a beautiful and pure devotion to Christ. While others may turn away to acquire possessions, prestige, or power, Rhea's father was wholly committed to Jesus. His confession echoes that of Peter's after Jesus had offered a difficult teaching. Scripture tells us that many of His disciples walked away and no longer followed Him (John 6:66). Jesus then asks those closest to Him if they would like to leave as well. Peter's response is so simple and sincere: "Lord, to whom shall we go?" (v. 68). Jesus was everything Peter needed.

The world will try to woo us with a variety of things. It will cause people to strive for financial security, man's applause, and physical comfort. If we can have Jesus and these things? All the better. But the Christian faith is not a "Jesus plus" faith. Following Jesus may just cost us our financial stability. Our devotion may make us no longer popular in certain circles. It will definitely call us out of our comfort zones. But He will always be worth it.

Lord, give me a heart that would rather have You.

42

The *love* of God
is greater far

Than tongue or
pen can ever tell;

It goes beyond
the highest *star*,

And *reaches* to
the lowest hell.

THE LOVE OF GOD

Growing up in small Southern churches, I spent many a Sunday morning and evening singing old hymns from a hymnal. Perhaps it's because I always had such a love for the written language, but I would get caught up in the lyrics to the songs and the stories behind them. Of all the beautiful songs, "The Love of God" has to be my favorite. I always thought it so overwhelming that the third verse was actually found scribbled on the walls of an insane asylum.

The story is told that, after an inmate named Frederick Lehman died, the asylum workers found it written on the wall of his room. Later, it was discovered to be a translation of an old Jewish poem. It is believed that, somehow, this person scratched it out in a rare moment of mental clarity. I can't help but be moved to tears by the thought that God, in His infinite grace and mercy, spoke through the chaos in this person's mind and whispered words of love to him.

It is a beautiful picture of the love of God described in Romans 8:39: "Nor height nor depth, nor any other created thing, shall be able to separate us from the love of God which is in Christ Jesus our Lord." We are never beyond the reach of God's love. It finds us in the deepest pit, the highest mountain, and even within the confines of a disturbed mind. Nothing shall ever separate us from the love of God.

> Your love, oh Lord, is the most precious thing
> to me, far greater than I can ever express.

43

I was sinking deep in sin, far
from the *peaceful* shore,

Very *deeply* stained within,
sinking to rise no more;

But the *Master* of the sea
heard my despairing cry,

From the *waters* lifted
me, now safe am I.

LOVE LIFTED ME

Scripture tells us of a time when the disciples were out on a boat in the middle of the night (Matthew 14:22–31). The winds and waves were strong, and the boat was in the middle of the sea instead of at shore. Jesus approached them, walking on the water toward the ship, and the disciples, at first, believed Him to be a ghost. After reassuring them, Jesus invited Peter to walk on the water toward Him. Peter did just that until he became afraid and began to sink. He cried out for help, and Jesus immediately reached out and caught Peter.

The biblical account found in Matthew was the inspiration behind James Rowe's hymn "Love Lifted Me." He likened a person apart from Christ to someone drowning in the middle of a sea. Just like Peter, a sinner is sinking without any way of saving himself, and the situation is dire. But at the sound of the sinner's cry, Jesus reaches out and lifts him to safety. The second verse then tells the hearer that Jesus can do the same for any soul in danger who calls on Him.

Rowe did an excellent job of using the story of Peter and Jesus in the middle of the sea as a beautiful picture of the gospel. All the sinner has to do is cry out to Jesus, and, because of His love, Jesus will hear the cry and completely save him from the depths to which he was sinking.

Thank You, Lord, for hearing my cry
and lifting me out of my sin.

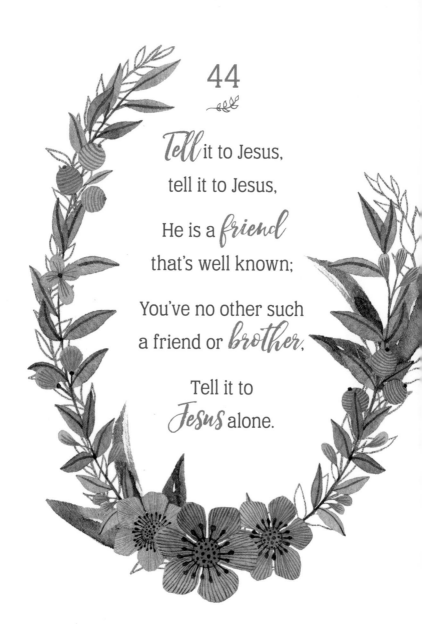

44

Tell it to Jesus,
tell it to Jesus,

He is a *friend*
that's well known;

You've no other such
a friend or *brother*,

Tell it to
Jesus alone.

TELL IT TO JESUS

Have you ever experienced a time when you desperately needed to talk to someone? Maybe you had just encountered a hardship or enjoyed an unexpected blessing, and you wanted to share the moment with someone. Perhaps you had people around you but no one who would really get what you were going through. Then there are also those times when Jesus is the only one we *need* to tell. There are some things that are best kept between us and our Savior.

In his hymn "Tell It to Jesus," Jeremiah E. Rankin described all the different things a person could share with Jesus. He described grief in the first stanza. Scripture certainly confirms that Jesus is very much familiar with earthly grief and can certainly understand our pain. The next stanza refers to our regrets over our sin. While Jesus never sinned, He is certainly full of mercy and forgiveness for all sinners.

Rankin went on in the third stanza to speak to fear of the future and general anxieties of life. We can tell our own concerns to Jesus as well. Finally, the hymn closes out with thoughts of death. And who better to share our concerns with than the one who tasted and conquered death? Whatever is on our hearts and minds today, we can tell it to Jesus. Just like the disciples told Jesus when they were troubled (Matthew 14:12), we, too, can bring our every concern to Him.

Lord, I am so grateful that You hear my prayers and that I can come to You with any hurt, heartache, or hallelujah.

45

Blessed *assurance*,

Jesus is mine!

Oh, what a foretaste

of *glory* divine!

Heir of salvation,

purchase of God,

Born of His *Spirit*,

washed in His blood.

BLESSED ASSURANCE

F anny Crosby wrote thousands of hymns under hundreds of pseudonyms. Many of them were, no doubt, written from specific experiences she had during her life. Other times she would hear a tune or be given one, and the words would just come to her. Such was the case with "Blessed Assurance." A fellow friend and musician had composed a tune, and, upon hearing it, the idea behind the hymn just formed.

In 1 Peter, the apostle Peter was speaking to people living in exile. They were far from home and experiencing trials and afflictions. He spoke to them of their love for Jesus, whom they could not see with their eyes but loved anyway. Peter said that these exiles had a joy that was inexpressible because of their hope in Christ (1 Peter 1:8). They had the assurance of salvation—a blessed assurance. Their souls were secure no matter what they experienced on earth.

Every believer today has that same blessed assurance. We, like the recipients of Peter's letter, experience hardships while living far from our heavenly home. We haven't seen Jesus with our eyes, but we love Him. We believe and have a joy that is inexpressible because, for those who love Jesus and long for His return, we have the certainty expressed in Crosby's song.

This assurance causes us to live differently, to tell His story, and to praise Him continually.

In You, Lord, I am truly happy and blessed.

46

I have *found* a
friend in Jesus,

He's ev'rything to me,

He's the *fairest* of ten
thousand to my soul;

The *Lily* of the Valley,

in Him alone I see

All I need to *cleanse* and
make me fully whole.

THE LILY OF THE VALLEY

Although not intentionally, Charles Fry was the leader of the Salvation Army's first brass band. A bricklayer by trade, he and his sons offered their services as bodyguards during a time when the Salvation Army experienced ridicule. The men would bring their instruments and, when not dealing with troublemakers, would draw in spectators with their music.

Fry found himself meditating on Song of Solomon 2:1 during a sermon by the Salvation Army's founder, William Booth, in 1881: "I am the rose of Sharon, and the lily of the valleys." The words of Scripture spoke to him of the relationship between a believer and Jesus. He then penned the lyrics to "The Lily of the Valley." The words speak to the intimacy one can experience with the Savior.

We have all, at some point in our lives, looked for love in the wrong places. Maybe in another person or by engaging in behavior that wasn't healthy for us. In a world in love with the idea of love, with dating apps and matchmaking businesses galore, we often miss out on the greatest love of all: Jesus. Fry understood the beauty of what he had in Christ. Jesus was, as he wrote, everything to him. That same intimacy and perfect love is available to each of us. Jesus is the fairest of ten thousand.

Lord, Your love is the sweetest love I have ever known. You are all I need.

47

Jesus
paid it all,
All to
Him I owe;

Sin had left a
crimson stain,
He *washed* it
white as snow.

JESUS PAID IT ALL

Have you ever had someone pay for something on your behalf? It's somewhat common these days for strangers to perform random acts of kindness. Perhaps you've done it yourself by paying for someone else's meal. In 2014 nearly four hundred people created a "pay it forward" chain in a Starbucks drive-through by purchasing the coffee for the person behind them. I dare say that, at some point, the good deed had become a guilt deed where people felt pressured to keep the streak going. But it all came to a halt when, at some point, someone said, "I'll just take the drink that someone already bought for me, thank you very much."

While sitting in a church service one morning, Elvina Hall began contemplating the massive debt we owe to God and what an exorbitant price Jesus paid to satisfy that debt. She quickly wrote the lyrics to "Jesus Paid It All" in her hymnbook and showed it to the pastor after the service. It just so happened that the church organist had recently shared with the pastor a new tune he had composed. His music and Hall's words were a perfect match.

In Paul's letter to the Galatians, he said it this way: "Christ has redeemed us from the curse of the law" (3:13). We owed a debt that we could never pay, and we were in a dire state. The cost for our sin was death. But in His great love for us, Jesus paid it all.

"Thank You" seems so inadequate,
Lord, but I say it all the same.

48

I know not why
God's *wondrous* grace

To me He hath
made known,

Nor why, unworthy,
Christ in *love*

Redeemed me
for His own.

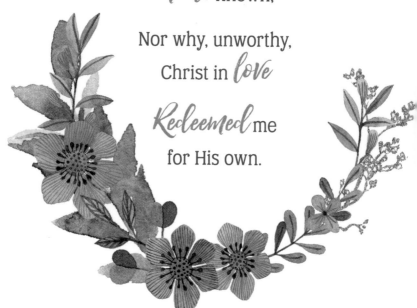

I KNOW WHOM I HAVE BELIEVED

I often say when leading Bible studies that we have to come to a place where we are okay not knowing what we are not meant to know. The precise moment of Christ's return is a great example. Although many speculate and debate, Scripture is clear that only the Father knows the time of Jesus' return (Matthew 24:36).

Daniel Whittle, the writer of "I Know Whom I Have Believed," understood that there were things he could not know. He readily admitted throughout the lyrics that he didn't know when the Lord would come for him. He couldn't explain how the Spirit moved in a man's heart or the peace he felt while reading Scripture. But the echoing refrain of the hymn reminds us that it isn't about *what* we know but *whom*.

There will be many times when we do not understand circumstances or trials we face. Paul wrote to Timothy the very words that this hymn is derived from during a time of affliction (2 Timothy 1:12). Paul told Timothy that he was suffering. He was in literal chains. Yet in the midst of his pain, he declared to Timothy that he knew Him whom he believed in, and he trusted Him with his life. We can have the same assurance that Paul and Whittle had. We can say with the saints of old, "I know whom I have believed."

Lord, I do not have to understand all the ways
You work to trust You with my life.

49

I need Thee,
O I *need* Thee;

Ev'ry *hour*
I need Thee!

O *bless* me now,
my Savior,

I come to *Thee*.

I NEED THEE EVERY HOUR

Have you ever attempted to do something for the Lord and failed miserably? Maybe it was a ministry you wanted to start at your church or a project you wanted to complete. If you're like me, you probably realized that you had forgotten to let the Lord be a part of the work you were trying to do. I certainly have been guilty of trying to do my own thing. I often need to be reminded of my need for Jesus.

It's true that many hymns were born of grief and torment. But when Annie Hawks wrote "I Need Thee Every Hour," she described it as being written and sent out into the world in love and joy. Honestly, it is one of the very few hymns that I have found to not stem from trials and tribulations in the writer's life. Perhaps it is because we are quick to forget the Lord during times of prosperity. We forget that we are as desperate for His presence and protection in the good times as we are in the bad. We would do well to remember that we do, in fact, need Christ every hour.

This song was based on Jesus' words in John 15:5. Jesus told the listeners that He was the vine and they were the branches. Apart from Him, Christ said, they could do nothing. This need to be constantly connected to the Lord was the essence of Hawks's hymn. She had an understanding of something that we often fail to comprehend. We need Jesus every hour of our lives.

Thank You, Lord, that when I stray too far, You have
a way of reminding me of my need for You.

50

Jesus is the
sweetest name I know,

And He's just the same
as His *lovely* name,

And that's the *reason*
why I love Him so;

Oh, Jesus is the sweetest
name I know.

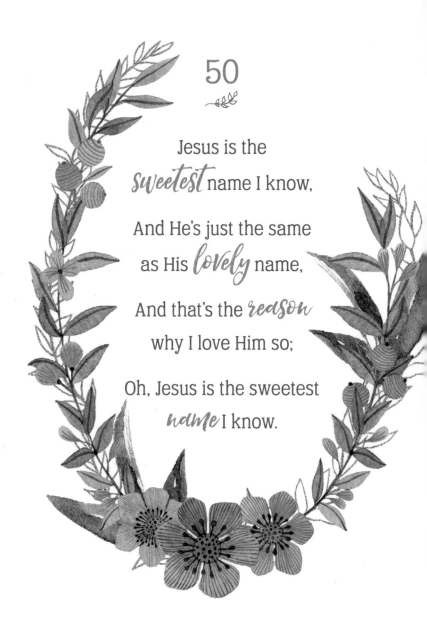

JESUS IS THE SWEETEST NAME I KNOW

Virtually nothing is known about hymn writer Lela B. Long except that, at some point in her life, she was inspired to record the words to "Jesus Is the Sweetest Name I Know." In other words, all we really know about her is how she felt about Jesus, which, perhaps, is the most important thing to know. Long's lyrics speak to an intimate relationship with the Savior. All earthly relationships must have paled in comparison.

A pastor of mine once said, when describing his feelings for Christ, "If there were no heaven, I would have loved Him anyway." Those words have remained in my heart and mind for more than twenty years. I have, at various points in my life, asked myself if those words were true for me. If there were no streets of gold or mansions on a hill—if all that eternity held was Jesus—would I love Him still? And the answer is a resounding, "Yes!"

Hebrews 13:8 tells us, "Jesus Christ is the same yesterday, today, and forever." It is believed that this was the verse that prompted Long to write the words, "He's just the same as His lovely name." Is there anything better than the sound of His name on your lips? His name is just as sweet and His love just as steadfast today as it was for Long over a century ago. And although we don't know when, one day every knee will bow at the sound of that sweet name.

Lord, You are everything to me. Your name
is truly the sweetest name I know.

51

Redeemed, how I
love to *proclaim* it!

Redeemed by the
blood of the *Lamb*;

Redeemed through
His infinite mercy,

His child, and *forever*, I am.

REDEEMED, HOW I LOVE TO PROCLAIM IT

Fanny Crosby wrote thousands of songs that Christians still enjoy today. However, she did not become a believer until the age of thirty when she was invited to a revival meeting by a friend. Although at first she did not wish to go, a disturbing dream convinced her to attend the meeting. At the end of the service, the choir sang a song by another famous hymnist, Isaac Watts, and Crosby was so moved by the hymn that she went forward and gave her life to Christ. She had gone to the altar a couple of times before, but this time there was a change within her heart.

Crosby would write many hymns over the course of her life describing her salvation experience and what it meant to her. She once said that the song that stood out to her the most was "Redeemed, How I Love to Proclaim It." It is no wonder that these lyrics would come to the forefront of her mind. How could someone not get excited when she is reminded that she is redeemed and loved by the Creator of the universe. Not only that, but also that He calls her "child"!

It is the same message that the psalmist sang long before the days of Crosby. In Psalm 107:2, the writer declared, "Let the redeemed of the Lord say so." Now it's our turn. If you've been redeemed, proclaim it.

I belong to You, Lord, and my lips can't help but tell it.

52

Lord, I *want* to
be a Christian
In my *heart*,
in my heart,

Lord, I want to
be a *Christian*

In *my*
heart.

LORD, I WANT TO BE A CHRISTIAN

It was the 1750s, and there were enslaved people working in the fields of Virginia. Exposed to the teaching of evangelist Samuel Davies, the weary and burdened people were inspired to sing. That is the origin of the African American spiritual "Lord, I Want to Be a Christian," and it is essential to know to fully appreciate this short but power-packed hymn.

Remarkably, the people enslaved on plantations in Virginia didn't sing about physical freedom for themselves or revenge on their enemies. Their songs were not of bitterness and woe. They weren't even dreaming about changes they desired to see in their harsh circumstances. The men and women sang about changes they wanted to see made in their own hearts.

> Lord, I want to be a Christian in my heart.
> Lord, I want to be more loving in my heart.
> Lord, I want to be more holy in my heart.
> Lord, I want to be like Jesus in my heart.

It may have been a sermon by Davies that inspired the lyrics, but only the Lord could change a person's heart (2 Corinthians 5:17). Only Jesus can give someone the desire to be more like Him. Whatever our trials, may our prayers be that we would be more like Jesus.

Lord, change my heart until I am more like You.

53

Grace, grace,
God's grace,

Grace that will *pardon*
and cleanse within;

Grace, grace,
God's grace,

Grace that is *greater*
than all our sin!

GRACE GREATER THAN OUR SIN

Grace is sometimes one of those overused and underappreciated words. In its most basic sense, grace is undeserved favor. Grace means being given or allowed to experience something good that we did not deserve and, therefore, had no reasonable expectation of receiving. It is the very essence of the gospel.

In eight short lines, Julia Johnston managed to describe the lavish grace of God toward His children. The first thing she said of it was that it was a grace that pardoned. In the legal world, a pardon has three essential elements. First, it can be done only by someone with executive power—a governor or a president. Second, the person being pardoned was, in fact, convicted of the crime. Third, the pardon removes any remaining punishment for the crime committed as well as preventing any future penalty for the same crime.

Ponder that concept for a moment as it relates to the grace of the gospel. Because of Jesus' sacrifice on our behalf, this is the grace in which believers now stand (Romans 5:2). God is the only one with the power to pardon. We were guilty, dead in our trespasses and sin (Colossians 2:13). Yet because of grace, the punishment is removed from us. That is God's grace. And it is, as Johnston wrote, greater than all our sin.

Lord, Your grace never ceases to amaze me.

54

Happy day, *happy* day,

When Jesus washed
my sins away!

He *taught* me how
to watch and pray,

And live *rejoicing* ev'ry day;

Happy day, happy day,

When Jesus washed
my sins *away*.

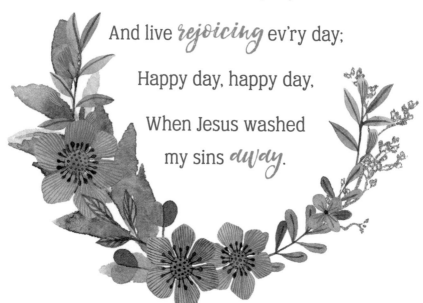

O HAPPY DAY THAT FIXED MY CHOICE

*C*an you recall the moment when you first realized your need for Jesus? Depending on how long ago it occurred, you may not remember all of the details, but you almost certainly remember the feeling. For me, to be honest, I don't remember the sermon or what it was that pricked my heart that day. What I can tell you with all certainty is how I felt. I knelt to pray at the altar, and when I arose, there was a lightness in my spirit that wasn't there before. It was a happy day.

The beauty of "O Happy Day That Fixed My Choice" is in its simplicity. Every believer sometimes needs a reminder of their own happy day with Jesus. Philip Doddridge was a pastor, poet, and brilliant scholar. He is most remembered, however, for his beautiful hymns, which weren't published until years after his death. Although written in the 1700s, the uplifting lyrics of "O Happy Day That Fixed My Choice" have continued to express the joy of salvation for generations.

The hymn was inspired by 2 Chronicles 15:15. The verse describes the moment when Judah rejoiced because they had sought the Lord, He was found by them, and He had given them rest. Judah rejoiced because it was a happy day. Take a moment and reminisce about the day when Jesus washed your sins away. Relive your own happy day.

Thank You, Lord, for the joy of salvation
and the happiness found in You.

55

O worship the *King*,
all glorious above,

And gratefully sing
His *wonderful* love;

Our *Shield* and Defender,
the Ancient of Days,

Pavilioned in *splendor*,
and girded with praise.

O WORSHIP THE KING

If you've been a Christian for any length of time, it has probably happened to you. Your faith becomes a bit of a routine. You've heard the stories. You've sung the songs. You know when to stand and when to sit during the church service. You do all the things, but you have, like the church in Ephesus, abandoned the love you had at first (Revelation 2:4). "O Worship the King" is the perfect hymn for when you find yourself in that place.

Robert Grant was inspired to write the lyrics to this song after hearing a paraphrase of Psalm 104. Both the psalm and hymn express praise and adoration for all that God is and all He has done. The psalmist opened his song by acknowledging God's greatness, splendor, and majesty and then spent thirty-five verses describing the magnificence of our Creator. Grant began with God's glory, strength, and eternal nature. He then went on, for five stanzas, to describe the care, love, and protection He provides.

Together, Psalm 104 and "O Worship the King" are the perfect cure for a heart that has grown a little casual toward God. They serve as beautiful reminders of His glory and splendor. Reading them on a regular basis will reignite the fire of our faith. It will give us back a little of the wonder that has, perhaps, slipped away from us. Let's take some time today to worship the King, all glorious above.

You, Lord, are so worthy of our praise and worship.

56

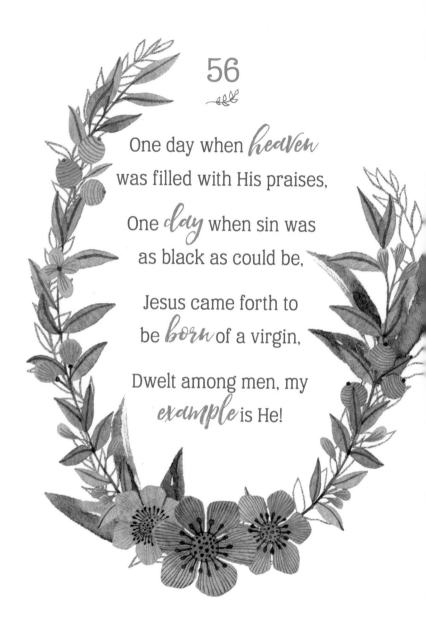

One day when *heaven*
was filled with His praises,

One *day* when sin was
as black as could be,

Jesus came forth to
be *born* of a virgin,

Dwelt among men, my
example is He!

ONE DAY

A lot of believers struggle with telling people about Jesus. What if someone has questions they can't answer? How can they share if they are short on time? There is a way to share the gospel in a concise and clear way. We see it in Scripture and in song.

The apostle Paul had an uncanny way of sharing the gospel in a simple, straightforward way. In his letter to Timothy, Paul explained the entire gospel in one verse about the "mystery of godliness" (1 Timothy 3:16). It included God coming in the flesh and being justified by the Spirit. He was seen by angels and preached among the Gentiles. Then, at the proper time, He was received in glory.

John Wilbur Chapman, a traveling evangelist in the late eighteenth century, wrote "One Day" based on those words from Paul. In the chorus of his hymn, Chapman managed to also share the mystery of godliness. In a few short lines, he addressed Jesus' life, death, and resurrection. It's a perfect outline for sharing the gospel with those around us.

The next time you have the opportunity to share with someone about Christ, think about the chorus of "One Day." Or maybe you need to remind yourself (as we sometimes do). He lived because He loved you. He died to save you. He rose, and, one day, He's coming again. O glorious day!

Lord, I long for the day You return. What
a wonderful day that will be!

57

Out in the *highways*
and byways of life,

Many are weary and sad;

Carry the *sunshine*
where darkness is rife,

Making the sorrowing *glad*.

MAKE ME A BLESSING

There are wounded people all around us. Many who cross our paths could use a helping hand. It is true that, as the opening lines of "Make Me a Blessing" state, many are weary and sad. There are numerous commands in Scripture for believers to assist the poor and needy among us. Romans 15:1 instructs those who are strong to help bear the burdens of the weak. We are called to love, encourage, and uplift the downtrodden. Unfortunately, busyness often blinds us to others and their needs.

Ira B. Wilson's words in "Make Me a Blessing" should echo the cry of every believer's heart. Although he was only twenty-nine when he wrote this hymn, the lyrics show a deep understanding of how the gospel looks when lived out. He wanted others to see Jesus in him. He wanted to share the power of Jesus' forgiveness. The final verse reiterates the call to love as Jesus loved (John 13:34).

There are countless ways we could be a blessing to those around us. We can help in tangible ways: take meals to the sick, sit with the lonely, run errands for the elderly. We can meet physical needs: do home repairs for widows, give financially to those in hardship, donate food to the hungry. But the greatest way we can be a blessing is to tell the sweet story of Christ and His love. Let's go be a blessing today.

Open my eyes, Lord, to the needs around
me every day. Make me a blessing.

58

Pass me not,
O *gentle* Savior,

Hear my

humble cry.

While on *others*
Thou art calling,

Do not
pass me by.

PASS ME NOT, O GENTLE SAVIOR

In Luke's gospel account, he told the story of a blind man in Jericho (Luke 18:35–38). The man sat on the roadside begging, which was most likely his regular practice. On one particular day, however, he heard the commotion of a large crowd and asked what it all meant. The people exclaimed that Jesus of Nazareth was passing by. Clearly, this meant something to the blind man because he cried out, "Jesus, Son of David, have mercy on me!"

This passage regarding the blind man inspired Fanny Crosby, who knew what it was like to live in darkness, to write "Pass Me Not, O Gentle Savior." How she must have identified with the man as he called out to Jesus. In her hymn, however, Crosby seemed to be referring to a different type of healing. The lyrics of this song are asking for the mercy and grace of Jesus in the face of a person's unbelief. The plea is for the healing of spiritual blindness.

The prophet Isaiah warned, "Seek the LORD while He may be found, call upon Him while He is near" (Isaiah 55:6). In other words, Jesus is passing by. Those who need their spiritual blindness healed can cry out to Him and He will hear them. Maybe it's you; don't be afraid to call upon Him. Perhaps you're one of the crowd who is already following Him. Are you telling others who can't see that Jesus is passing by?

Thank You, Lord, for not passing me by.

59

Praise God, from whom
all *blessings* flow;
Praise Him, all
creatures here below;

Praise Him above,
ye heav'nly *host*;

Praise Father, Son,
and *Holy* Ghost.

Amen.

PRAISE GOD, FROM WHOM ALL BLESSINGS FLOW

To what do you credit the good things in life that you enjoy? It's common to believe that hard work or good fortune is behind it all. Some would even go so far as to say that they deserve all the blessings that have come their way. The reality is that every good and perfect gift comes from God (James 1:17). Once we realize this truth, the only appropriate response is praise.

"Praise God, from Whom All Blessings Flow," often called the Doxology, was written by Thomas Ken. Ken was a chaplain to Princess Mary in The Hague and later a bishop. He was known for standing up for his religious convictions even if it meant a confrontation with royalty. Many churches, like the one I attend, sing Ken's hymn at the conclusion of their services. It is a reminder that anything good we may receive has come directly from the hand of God.

This is one of those hymns that is easy to memorize. We can sing the words by heart as we gather up our belongings at the end of a church service without even realizing what we are singing. I have certainly been guilty of that. Can I encourage you to take a moment and just read the words? Read them slowly and aloud. Remind yourself of how gracious the Lord has been in your life.

Lord, You have been so very good to me. Thank
You for Your good and perfect gifts.

60

Shall we gather
at the river,

Where bright
angel feet have trod;

With its crystal
tide forever

Flowing by the
throne of God?

SHALL WE GATHER AT THE RIVER

When I take my children somewhere that we know will be crowded, we discuss the possibility of separation. They know where to go if, for some reason, they find themselves away from me. They know to look for helpers, such as employees or police officers. We have the same discussion regarding emergencies. If there were a fire at our home and they were separated from us or one another, we have a place where everyone is to go. In every scenario, there is always a meeting place where the family will all gather.

This is the image that comes to mind when I hear "Shall We Gather at the River." Robert Lowry gives a beautiful word picture of Revelation 22:1: "And he showed me a pure river of water of life, clear as crystal, proceeding from the throne of God and of the Lamb." Written in 1864, the song has been loved for generations and was sung live at the funeral of American Supreme Court Justice William O. Douglas in 1980. I can't help but wonder what Lowry was imagining as he penned the lyrics. It is, as he wrote, the perfect gathering place for the saints of God.

It's always good to have a plan in place. If I get separated from my loved ones on earth, they will know where to look for me. We will gather at the river that flows by the throne of God. It will be easy to find; they can just listen for the sound of praise.

Lord, I can't wait to gather with the
saints around Your throne.

61

Sing the wondrous *love* of Jesus,

Sing His mercy and His grace;

In the *mansions* bright and blessed,

He'll prepare for us a *place*.

WHEN WE ALL GET TO HEAVEN

Eliza Edmunds Hewitt was born and raised in Philadelphia. She married a Methodist minister and spent a great deal of her time doing work within the church and community. While homebound due to a spinal issue, Hewitt studied literature and wrote hundreds of pieces. One of those pieces describes the grandest family reunion ever. It tells of a time when all believers will finally be together in heaven.

I was one of twelve cousins growing up. We were lovingly nicknamed the Dirty Dozen by my grandmother. My favorite day of the year was Thanksgiving. That was the time that our entire family gathered at my aunt's house and had a family reunion of sorts. Those Thanksgivings stand out in my memory as days of joy, but those days will pale in comparison to the day Hewitt described in "When We All Get to Heaven." No doubt we all have loved ones waiting for us in glory.

This hymn gives us some important lessons about heaven based in Scripture. It reminds us that Jesus is, in fact, preparing us a place (John 14:2). We can know that this place He is preparing for us is a place of joy. And one day there will be a grand reunion of the saints in that place. What a day of rejoicing that will be!

Thank You, Lord, for the beautiful glimpses
of heaven found in Scripture.

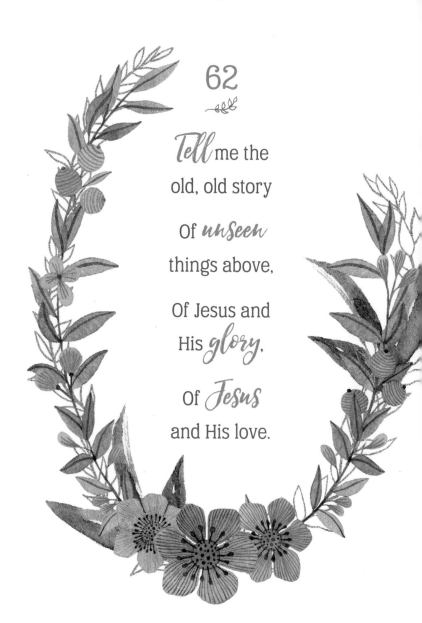

62

Tell me the
old, old story

Of *unseen*
things above,

Of Jesus and
His *glory*,

Of *Jesus*
and His love.

TELL ME THE OLD, OLD STORY

Have you ever thought about what stories you would want Jesus to tell you? For all the miracles we read about in Scripture, there are countless others that were not included. John tells us, in his gospel account, that there were many signs performed that were not included in his book (John 20:30). But even of those included in Scripture, we all certainly have our favorites. (Mine would be any story involving Peter.) Could you imagine Jesus Himself telling your favorite to you?

"Tell Me the Old, Old Story" is taken from a portion of a much longer poem about the life of Christ written by Katherine Hankey. (Another part of that same poem was used to write the hymn "I Love to Tell the Story.") In the poem, she mentioned the tales she would ask Jesus Himself to tell if He was there to do so. She referred to stories of the sea, of children gathered around His knee, and of His acts of grace. For Hankey, it was the old, old story that never grew old.

As a child, I kept a small journal in which I would write the questions that I wanted to ask Jesus one day. Maybe you've had questions as well. The more I walk with the Lord, however, the more in agreement I am with Hankey. I don't need a question-and-answer time with the Lord because my earthly concerns will no longer matter. I can just sit at Jesus' feet as He tells me a story.

Lord, I cannot wait to hear the old, old
story from Your precious lips.

63

There is a *name*
I love to hear,

I love to sing
its *worth*;

It *sounds* like
music in my ear,

The sweetest
name on *earth*.

OH, HOW I LOVE JESUS

Maybe for you it is the name of a spouse. Perhaps it is the name of a child or grandchild. The specific person may be different for each of us, but we all have someone whose very name warms our hearts and makes us smile. For me, the sweetest name of all is that of Jesus. There is actually an entire subset of hymns that are solely about His name.

Frederick Whitfield's hymn "Oh, How I Love Jesus" may be one of the simplest and most sincere songs of all time. Born in the early 1800s, Whitfield went to school in Dublin and was ordained in the Church of England. At the height of his career, he received an assignment at St. Mary's Church in Hastings. Among his thirty volumes of writing was this hymn of praise to the name of Jesus.

Scripture tells us that, at the name of Jesus, every knee will bow in heaven, on earth, and under the earth (Philippians 2:10). Paul made it clear that the name of Jesus is a powerful name. Yet for those of us who love Jesus, His name is also precious. It is the only name by which we can be saved. It is the only name that makes demons flee. Just the sound of it brings comfort in times of sorrow. It is, as Whitfield described, the sweetest name on earth.

Your name is precious to me, Lord. Oh, how I love You.

64

Send the light, the
blessed *gospel* light;

Let it *shine* from
shore to shore!

Send the light, the
blessed gospel light;

Let it shine
forevermore!

SEND THE LIGHT

There is a point in time for every Christ follower when he or she leaves the darkness and enters the light. But how can people know about the light if they are not told (Romans 10:14)? It could've happened anywhere, but the fact remains that somebody sent the light your way. It's the way God designed the gospel to spread; believers are to go and tell.

Charles Gabriel's hymn "Send the Light" is a sober reminder of the importance of sharing the gospel with the people around us.

> There are souls to rescue.
> There are souls to save.

Jesus told a parable about His people bringing light to the world. In that parable He said, "No one, when he has lit a lamp, covers it with a vessel or puts it under a bed, but sets it on a lampstand, that those who enter may see the light" (Luke 8:16). Notice that Jesus didn't say it was unusual to put a lamp under a bed. He was clear that no one would do such a thing. It would be foolish, wasteful, and dangerous.

The gospel is our lit lamp. Let's send it everywhere until no one is living in darkness.

> Let my life be a light, Lord. May I shine the
> light of Your love everywhere I go.

65

O come, all ye faithful,
joyful and triumphant!

O come ye, O come
ye to Bethlehem;

Come and *behold* him

Born the King of Angels:

O *come*, let us
adore Him,

Christ the *Lord*!

O COME, ALL YE FAITHFUL

Christmas carols are among some of the most beloved hymns. Originally written in Latin by John Francis Wade in the mid 1700s, "O Come, All Ye Faithful" is a favorite of many. The hearers of Wade's penned verses are invited to journey with the shepherds as they make their way to Bethlehem to meet the newborn king. Luke tells the story, in his gospel account, of the angels appearing to the shepherds and announcing the birth of Christ. In response, the shepherds said, "Let us now go to Bethlehem and see this thing that has come to pass, which the Lord has made known to us" (Luke 2:15).

In an even greater way, the song invites all believers to come and behold him. The faithful, joyful, and triumphant are all welcome to come and adore the One born in Bethlehem. While the song begins by referencing the earthly arrival of the baby Jesus, the second stanza makes clear that Wade believed in the deity of Jesus as well. "God of God," He wrote. "Very God, begotten not created."

And therein lies the miracle of the Christmas story. It's the reason the angels sang in exultation. God, very God, had entered a virgin's womb and had come to earth in the form of an infant. No wonder the shepherds had to see for themselves. It's a story worth celebrating all year long. Let's not miss a single opportunity to adore Him.

Lord, I come with the faithful to adore You. Thank You for the opportunity to celebrate You.

66

There's not a *friend*
like the lowly Jesus,

No, not one!
No, not one!

None else could *heal*
all our soul's diseases,

No, not *one*!
No, not one!

NO, NOT ONE

Have you ever expected too much from someone? We do that sometimes, don't we? It's easy to place unrealistic expectations on people and then be disappointed when they fall short. We want people to be exactly what we need them to be at all times. We expect them to understand our struggles and anticipate our needs. Basically, we try to make people be for us what only Jesus was meant to be. The problem is that there is no one like Jesus. No, not one.

Although an ordained minister, Johnson Oatman Jr. spent his adult years working first in his father's business and then working in life insurance. His father's love of music, however, clearly rubbed off on him as he wrote over three thousand hymns during the course of his lifetime. "No, Not One," written by Oatman, is a beautiful reminder that there is no one like Jesus. It's trite but true that, just when you think He's all you have, you'll find He's all you need. No one knows you more intimately than the Lord, and no one loves you more sincerely.

Jesus gets you. He knows about your struggles and can sympathize with you (Hebrews 4:15). He can heal you, He will guide you, and He promises to never leave your side. There is no other friend who can make and keep such promises to us.

What a friend I have in You, Lord. No
other can ever take Your place.

67

Were you *there* when
they crucified my Lord?

Were you there when they
crucified my *Lord*?

Oh, sometimes it causes me to
tremble, tremble, tremble.

Were *you* there when
they crucified my Lord?

WERE YOU THERE

I have a hard and fast rule when it comes to music and movies. I don't want to hear or watch anything sad. Give me the inspirational, funny, and even scary, but I'll pass on anything that requires tissues. Life is too short to spend my time thinking about lost love or sinking ships. Sometimes, however, I can push through the sad part of the story when I know the end makes it all worth it. "Were You There" is a perfect example.

Although not published until 1889, this African American spiritual predates the Civil War. Three out of the four stanzas have a decidedly dark and somber tone as the words call to mind the death of Christ. "Were you there," it asks, "when they crucified my Lord?" "Were you there when they nailed Him to the tree?" "Were you there when they laid Him in the tomb?" The music is deep and slow. The emotion builds and the tears well. It would only be a sad song, though, if the third verse was the last.

Every time I listen to "Were You There," I tell myself, "You can't have the resurrection without the crucifixion." To truly rejoice in the risen Savior, we must look in the face of the crucified One. We must be with Him in the garden, walk with Him up the hill, and feel the weight of the cross. Only then can we experience the fourth verse, which celebrates when God raised Him from the tomb. It's a story worth singing every time.

What a sacrifice You made for me,
Lord. It causes me to tremble.

68

Since Jesus came
into my *heart,*

Since *Jesus*
came into my heart,

Floods of joy o'er my soul
like the *Sea* billows roll,

Since Jesus came
into my heart.

SINCE JESUS CAME INTO MY HEART

Rufus McDaniel's goal in life was to be a blessing to struggling souls. Specifically, he felt called to do so by writing hymns. He found so much joy through music that he wanted to share it with others. Based on the number of people still singing his songs today, McDaniel certainly succeeded in blessing others with his gift of song.

Written in 1914, "Since Jesus Came into My Heart" describes the change that occurs when someone experiences the cleansing and forgiveness of Christ. There is a joy that comes with such a change. It's a joy that, once experienced, you'll never want to be without. It's what David missed so dearly after sinning with Bathsheba. He didn't ask for his salvation to be restored, because that was never lost. David asked for God to restore his joy (Psalm 51:12).

The first time I met Sara, it was clear that life had weighed her down. She was stressed and weary, and she looked the part. There was a harshness about her that was off-putting and intimidating. One day our paths crossed, and we paused to chat. Immediately, I knew something was different. She was open and friendly. When I asked about the change, she said, "It's the joy of the Lord." She had realized her need for Jesus, had spoken to a local pastor, and now had joy flooding her soul. McDaniel had it right; that's what happens when Jesus comes into your heart.

Your joy, Lord, is life-changing. May
others see Your joy in me.

69

When we *walk* with the Lord

In the *light* of His Word

What a glory He
sheds on our *way*!

While we do His *good* will;

He *abides* with us still,

And with all who will
trust and obey.

TRUST AND OBEY

What is the most difficult thing the Lord has ever asked you to do? For some people it may be forgiving someone who wasn't sorry. Or putting someone else's needs ahead of your own. Maybe you have felt called to a mission field far from home. Often the difficult part isn't discerning the will of God but deciding to trust Him and obey.

During a revival meeting held by Dwight L. Moody, a new believer was heard telling someone, "I am going to trust and obey." Professor Towner, who worked for the Moody Institute, together with John Sammis, took that heartfelt sentiment and wrote "Trust and Obey." The concept behind it is simple to understand but, often, more difficult to live out. Much like Paul, we don't understand why we do the things we don't want to do and fail to do things we know are right (Romans 7:15).

Trusting and obeying are keys to living a life that pleases the Lord. There will be times when it is easier, and other times it will take courage and faith. People will not always agree with or understand the things we do. Some will mock and seek to discourage us. David's encouragement in such situations was to "Trust in the LORD, and do good" (Psalm 37:3). In other words, "Trust and obey."

Lord, give me a heart that trusts and obeys at all times.

70

Crown him with
many crowns,

The Lamb upon
his throne;

Hark! how the heav'nly
anthem drowns

All music
but its own.

CROWN HIM WITH MANY CROWNS

Written by Matthew Bridges, "Crown Him with Many Crowns" was inspired by Revelation 19:12: "His eyes were like a flame of fire, and on His head were many crowns. He had a name written that no one knew except Himself." It presents an image of Jesus being given all the honor and glory due Him.

Bridges hailed Jesus as the perfect Lamb who was sacrificed to appease the wrath of a holy God. He then acknowledged Jesus as the Lord of life. The one who conquered the grave and defeated death deserves to wear the crown. Jesus is then called the Lord of love. Scripture makes it clear that there is no greater love than to lay down your life for someone else (John 15:13), and that is exactly what Christ did on the cross.

Finally, Jesus is crowned the Lord of years. He is the one who exists from "in the beginning" to eternity.

Is there any area of your life that you have not yet turned over to King Jesus? A part that you haven't quite let go of yet? To call Him Lord means that He reigns over every area of our lives. Any control we believe we have is a façade, and we waste energy trying to cling to it. Jesus is worthy of our trust and devotion.

Lord, search my heart, and reveal to me any area of my life not fully submitted to You.

71

When I *survey* the
wondrous cross

On which the
Prince of glory died,

My *richest* gain
I count but loss,

And *pour* contempt
on all my pride.

WHEN I SURVEY THE WONDROUS CROSS

W hat are you tempted to be prideful about? Maybe financial prosperity, career success, or social media influence? From a worldly perspective, Paul had plenty worthy of boasting about. He described himself as circumcised on the eighth day, of the people of Israel, of the tribe of Benjamin, a Hebrew of Hebrews, and faultless in regard to keeping the law. Yet Paul made it clear that he would only boast in what Christ did on the cross (Galatians 6:14).

Isaac Watts echoed Paul's sentiment in his hymn "When I Survey the Wondrous Cross." In the second verse, Watts wrote that he would only boast in the death of Christ. He would not take pride in earthly accomplishments or possessions. It's a beautiful reminder of the magnitude of what Christ did on the cross, and the song is, ironically, considered Watts's highest achievement.

The power of hymns is found in their deep connection to Scripture. It is what causes the words to be sung for generations. This moving hymn ends with a commitment to give Christ our soul, our life, our all. It is what Jesus called the greatest commandment—to love the Lord with all our hearts, souls, and minds (Matthew 22:37). It is a fitting response to the work of Christ. All of our works pale in comparison to the wondrous cross.

Lord, may I never lose sight of what
You accomplished on the cross.

72

Amazing Grace!
how sweet the sound,

That *saved* a
wretch like me!

I once was lost, but
now am *found*,

Was blind,
but *now* I see.

AMAZING GRACE

What kind of music appeals to you? My husband and I often say that we are drawn to music sung by people who lived the lyrics—for instance, Willie Nelson singing about being on the road again or Eric Clapton longing to see someone in heaven. It's moving and believable because they're authentically singing about something they experienced.

John Newton knew what he was talking about when he wrote the words to "Amazing Grace." He knew where he had been and what he had done. Prior to becoming a Christian, Newton was the captain on a slave ship. It took a near-death experience, the faithful witness of his wife, and some literature on the life of Christ to result in his conversion. He then joined forces with William Wilberforce and became an abolitionist. His hymn shows that, like Paul before him (Romans 7:24), Newton was very much aware of his own wretchedness. He lived his lyrics.

While Newton's slave-trader-to-salvation story and Paul's murderer-to-missionary testimony are exceptional, the grace given to you or me is no less amazing. It is an absolute miracle that anyone would be saved. We were all wretched, lost, and blind before Christ. There is no one worthy of salvation, and that is why "Amazing Grace" has resonated with believers for over two hundred years.

Your grace, Lord, never ceases to amaze me.

73

Holy, holy, *holy*!

Lord *God*
Almighty!

Early in the

morning

our *song* shall
rise to Thee.

HOLY, HOLY, HOLY

The hymn "Holy, Holy, Holy" is unique in that it isn't a call to praise or worship. Instead it is an invitation to join in on the praise already and continually taking place around the throne in heaven (Revelation 4:8). It's a song that doesn't end—day or night. Through the pen of Reginald Heber, we can add our voices to those currently echoing in glory. His song is a reminder that worship isn't something we do on a Sunday morning; it's something we do day in and day out.

Heber is considered a hero of the faith. He was born into a wealthy family in England but ended up as Bishop of Calcutta. He was ahead of his time in the way his ministry and music crossed racial and geographical boundaries. It is fitting then that the vision given to John in Revelation revealed "Holy, Holy, Holy" to be the soundtrack of heaven. Every tribe and tongue will be singing it around the throne. What an experience it must have been for Heber to join in with them.

One day all who know Christ as Lord and Savior will join in on that heavenly hymn. We will praise Him with angels and the saints who have gone on before us. We won't need to come up with anything original. No other words will be necessary, just "holy, holy, holy."

Lord, You are holy and worthy of all my praise.

74

Be Thou my *Vision*,
O Lord of my heart;

Naught be all else to
me, save that Thou art.

Thou my best thought,
by *day* or by night,

Waking or sleeping, Thy
presence my *light*.

BE THOU MY VISION

What is the biggest hindrance to your living wholeheartedly for the Lord? What stops you from passionately pursuing all of the spiritual disciplines? For most of us the answer is not that complicated. We simply have a whole lot of distractions. Our focus is easily taken away from God and placed on other things. Our vision is clouded by worldly pleasures and pursuits.

"Be Thou My Vision" is credited to an Irish monk named Dallan Forgaill from the sixth century who wrote the poem in honor of St. Patrick. Hundreds of years later Mary Elizabeth Byrne translated it into English. In 1912 it was put into hymn form by Eleanor Hull. In other words, a lot of individuals had a hand in producing the song as we know it today. What makes any work get passed on for more than a thousand years? Maybe because the plea behind it spoke to people in every century.

Prone-to-wander hearts are nothing new. Believers have struggled to be faithful since the beginning. "Be Thou My Vision" is a request for God to help us focus (and refocus) our gaze on Him. To remove distractions. To help us seek Him above everything else. To take the directive from the author of Hebrews and "fix our eyes on Jesus" (Hebrews 12:2 NIV). We can't do it on our own, and so it's a good thing we're not on our own.

Remove all the distractions, Lord, so
that I can be devoted to You.

75

Take the *world*,

but give me Jesus,

All its joys are

but a *name*;

But His *love*

abideth ever,

Through eternal

years the same.

GIVE ME JESUS

What have you seen someone give up or walk away from for Jesus? Maybe it was financial stability or physical comfort. Perhaps it was someone giving up on the way he or she thought their life would go and trusting Jesus in the place He had them. It may look like no longer striving for worldly success. Ultimately, it comes down to making a choice between Jesus and whatever the world happens to offer.

In yet another well-loved hymn by Fanny Crosby, she made her choice quite clear: "Give me Jesus." Throughout the hymn, Crosby described the benefits of choosing Jesus. She would rather have His love, His comfort, and His smile as she made her way through life. She had a clear understanding of what truly mattered. She understood that it would profit her nothing to gain the world but not have Jesus (Mark 8:36).

While it sounds pretty in rhyming words on paper, it takes a strong faith to choose the Lord daily—to believe that what He has in store for you is better. Crosby believed this, and it enabled her to see Jesus at work even in her blindness. The affliction helped to give her time to pursue education, and gain influence, as well as improve her memory. By the age of ten, she had committed four Old Testament books and the four Gospels to memory. We can learn from Crosby's example. When the choices are laid out before us, let's choose Jesus every time.

Lord, this world has nothing that compares with You.
May the cry of my heart always be, "Just give me Jesus."

76

God moves in a
mysterious way

His *wonders*
to perform;

He plants his
footsteps in the *Sea*,

And *rides*
upon the storm.

GOD MOVES IN A
MYSTERIOUS WAY

M ost of us are more likely to praise the Lord when we have been rescued from a trial or have avoided a potentially difficult situation. Mountaintop experiences often bring out the praises while we sometimes struggle to understand the valleys.

William Cowper, the author of "God Moves in a Mysterious Way," knew about loss and heartache. He was intimately acquainted with darkness and despair. He lost his mother at a young age and was sent to a boarding school by his father. As an adult, he struggled with bouts of depression and suicidal ideations. Cowper became a believer while residing in an insane asylum when he crossed paths with a doctor who loved God and shared the gospel message with him.

These are the questions that have been asked for ages: Why do bad things happen to good people? Why do some seem to suffer while others prosper? The only answer available to us is that His ways are not like ours. There will always be things that our finite minds aren't able to understand. God moves in mysterious ways that are beyond our comprehension. In those moments, we place our faith in His goodness and steadfast love.

Your ways are higher than my ways, Lord.
Help me to trust when I don't understand.

77

Peace, peace!
wonderful peace,

Coming down from
the Father *above*,

Sweep over my *spirit*
forever, I pray,

In *fathomless*
billows of love.

WONDERFUL PEACE

In 1889 pastor and evangelist Warren Cornell attended a camp meeting in Michigan, led by Reverend William Cooper. Following a period of meditation, long after the others had gone, Cornell had jotted down some lines describing the peace of God in the heart of the believer. When he left, Cornell inadvertently left the piece of paper behind. A few hours later, Pastor Cooper entered the tent, spotted the piece of paper, and became inspired by the words, which appeared to be part of a poem. He not only completed the poem but also wrote the music to accompany the verses, which is how the song "Wonderful Peace" came to be.

Sometimes we have the time and mental energy to tackle large portions of Scripture. Other times we wake up feeling as though we are already running behind before the day has begun. The tough days are the days we need it most—even if we meditate on only one facet, just as Pastor Cornell had done more than a century ago.

Whatever you are dealing with, whatever wound is not yet healed, just remember this beautiful truth to cling to for those of us who love God's Word: We are promised great peace. What would great and wonderful peace look like for us? Maybe it's trusting God to handle the circumstance we've been trying so hard to control.

Sometimes we struggle simply because we don't access the things promised to us. Let's not spend another day without the great peace of our heavenly Father.

Thank You, Lord, for the precious peace available in You.

78

Breathe on me,
Breath of God,

Fill me with
life anew,

That I may love what
Thou dost *love*,

And *do* what
Thou wouldst do.

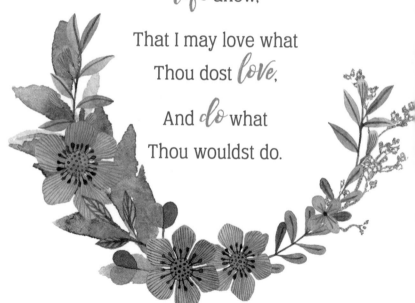

BREATHE ON ME, BREATH OF GOD

You are, most likely, completely aware of your need to breathe. It is essential for life, and it takes only a few seconds underwater to be reminded of the fact. Have you ever considered that the breath of God that gave you life is also necessary for your spiritual life?

Unlike many of the hymn writers of his day who wrote prolifically, Edwin Hatch only wrote a few songs, including "Breathe on Me, Breath of God." In the three short verses of this hymn, he expressed how necessary the breath of God is in a person's life. Although highly educated, the simplicity of the lyrics reflected his faith.

The breath of God is a theme throughout all of Scripture. Genesis shows that man, although handmade by a holy God, did not live until He breathed life into him (Genesis 2:7). That's probably not news to anyone, but Hatch's words remind us that same breath is also needed for "life anew." It's the lesson given by the prophet Ezekiel when he is shown the vision of the valley of dry bones (Ezekiel 37). Then, in the New Testament, there is the account of Jesus breathing on the disciples in the upper room.

Although the hymn may be short and the word choice simplistic, "Breathe on Me" reveals the necessity and consistency of the breath of God throughout Scripture. It is necessary for giving, renewing, and maintaining life. What area of your life needs the breath of God today?

Thank You, Lord, for the breath that gives
physical, spiritual, and eternal life.

79

I will sing of the mercies
of the Lord *forever*,

I will *sing*, I will sing,

What a mercy that I am in
the *church* forever,

I will sing of the
mercies of the Lord.

I WILL SING OF THE MERCIES OF THE LORD

*C*omposer James Henry Fillmore, who sometimes used the pseudonym Harold Bennett, composed this hymn based on Psalm 89.

Mercy and forgiveness often accompany each other. Mercy means showing compassion or forbearance, especially to someone who has committed an offense. Forgiveness isn't pretending that a wrong was never committed. In the Lord's Prayer, the model prayer for believers, Jesus told His disciples two specific things regarding what forgiveness would look like in real life.

First, we are called to forgive everyone. This includes those who don't ask for our forgiveness and those who don't feel like they need it. We are to forgive those who we feel don't deserve it as well as those who can never undo what has been done. Jesus didn't add any exceptions or qualifiers in His reference to forgiveness. *Everyone* meant everyone.

Second, we are to forgive those who are currently indebted to us. Jesus didn't say, "You need to forgive them because what they did wasn't that bad anyway." Forgiving them means we no longer hold that debt against them. Mercy adds the element of compassion and blessing, which goes just one step beyond basic forgiveness.

This song reminds us of Jesus' capacity to forgive and show mercy to us, and that this spirit of forgiveness lives in us.

Lord, help us to forgive like You forgive and show mercy like You show mercy.

80

Away in a manger,
no crib for a bed,

The little Lord Jesus laid
down His *sweet* head;

The *stars* in
the *heavens* looked
down where He lay,

The little Lord Jesus
asleep on the hay.

AWAY IN A MANGER

"Away in a Manger" is one of the first Christmas carols many of us learned. We all know it by heart and probably give little thought to the words. Although sometimes attributed to Martin Luther, many believe that the true author is unknown. Either way, the lyrics fill us with childlike wonder as we envision the birth of Jesus, but we would be remiss to write this hymn off as only for children.

A reference to the baby in the manger as the Lord Jesus gives an accurate picture of His humanity and deity intertwined. The fact that He had no crib for a bed is only truly appreciated if we realize that He had a throne in heaven. He once looked down on the stars, and now the stars looked down on Him. He left a place where He was surrounded by the praises of the heavenly host to come to earth and be surrounded by the lowing of cattle.

The miracle of the Christmas story is that God wrapped Himself in flesh and came to earth in the womb of a teenage girl. The wonder is that He voluntarily left the splendor and glory of heaven to do it. The Christmas story is for believers of all ages. We are never too old to sing about the baby in the manger.

Lord, may we always feel the
wonder of the Christmas story.

81

Great is Thy *faithfulness*,
O God, my Father;
There is no shadow of
turning with Thee;

Thou changest not, Thy
compassions, they fail not;
As *Thou* hast been,
Thou forever wilt be.

GREAT IS THY FAITHFULNESS

How has God shown Himself faithful throughout your lifetime? What does your personal hymn sound like? We could certainly all fill a book with our own personal experiences. He has healed bodies, saved marriages, comforted the lonely, and provided financially. He has been a friend to the friendless and a Father to the fatherless. Take a moment and meditate on God's faithfulness to you personally.

Thomas O. Chisholm wrote "Great Is Thy Faithfulness" to express his praise and adoration for God's faithfulness over his lifetime. He became a Christian at the age of twenty-six and entered the ministry a few years later. Chisholm wanted his writing to be rich in theology and void of sentimentalism. He certainly achieved that with this work. The words are taken directly from the words of Jeremiah in Lamentations 3:23.

The lyrics speak to the unchanging, omnipresent, compassionate nature of our God. They remind us that He never leaves or forsakes us. It closes with the promise of the Lord's pardon, peace, and presence. While the details of our stories may all be different, the theme of God's faithfulness runs through them all. We could all look back over our walk with the Lord and proclaim, "Great is Thy faithfulness."

Thank You, Lord, for Your faithfulness
to me through the years.

82

Come, thou
Almighty King,

Help us Thy name to sing,

Help us to praise.

Father, all glorious,

O'er all *Victorious*,

Come, and reign over us,

Ancient of Days.

COME, THOU ALMIGHTY KING

This anonymous hymn, written in the 1700s, is considered a Trinitarian prayer because of its references to all three members of the Trinity. The first stanza speaks to God the Father. He is praised as glorious, victorious, and eternal. The second verse heralds the Son as the One on whom our souls are dependent. He is the Word incarnate (John 1:1). Jesus was with God in the beginning, then He became flesh and dwelt among us.

Then, in the third verse, the author calls upon the Holy Spirit to take up residence and rule in every heart. It is the Comforter promised to us by Jesus (John 14:16). He is the source of conviction and power in our lives.

Finally, the hymn concludes with praises for the Trinity as a whole. The writer looks forward to the day he will see the triune God with his own eyes.

The Trinity is a glorious mystery. Every believer has, at some point, attempted to explain it to someone or to themselves. It is one of the many ways God's thoughts and ways are higher than ours. This hymn, however, brilliantly breaks it down and reminds us of the glory and holiness of our God.

Lord, You are worthy of all honor
and glory and praise.

83

"Take up your *cross*,"
the Savior said,

"If you would My
disciple be;

Take up your cross
with willing *heart*,

And humbly
follow after Me."

TAKE UP YOUR CROSS

Dietrich Bonhoeffer once said, "When Christ calls a man, He bids him come and die." It is the essence of the life of a believer. We die to our own fleshly wants and desires, and we choose, instead, to pursue only the things of God. The life of a Christian is one of self-denial.

Jesus made it clear that a life devoted to Him would be a life of sacrifice. He told the disciples that each of them must pick up his cross and follow Him (Matthew 16:24). We all have our own individual crosses to bear as well. It's tempting to look at someone else and think that his or her cross is somehow lighter than ours, but in reality, someone else's cross appears lighter only because someone else is carrying it.

This is the essence of Charles Everest's hymn "Take Up Your Cross." He described the humiliation, weight, and shame of the cross—and encouraged believers to bear the weight of it anyway. It is a weight, of course, that we could never bear on our own. But Everest's lyrics remind us that Jesus helps bear this weight. Our Lord strengthens our spirits and our bodies so that we are able to follow Him wherever He leads.

What load are you being asked to bear today? Maybe it is a difficult marriage, a child with an illness, or a prodigal loved one. Whatever your cross looks like, Jesus will help you carry it.

Lord, give me the strength I need to
follow You wholeheartedly.

84

By and by when the
morning comes,

When the *saints* of God
are gathered home,

We'll tell the story how
we've *overcome*;

For we'll *understand*
it better by and by.

WE'LL UNDERSTAND IT BETTER BY AND BY

*T*hings happen in life that do not make sense to our human, finite minds. Children get sick, war breaks out, and some people seem to struggle every day of their existence. We don't understand, and our flesh cries out, "Why, Lord?" When asked about all the affliction he had seen, a missionary once said that our question in heaven will not be, "Why all the suffering?" It will instead be, "What suffering?" Because, as Paul said, all of our trials and tribulations will pale in comparison to the glory we will experience (2 Corinthians 4:17).

There were plenty of things about Charles Albert Tindley's life that surely didn't make sense to him. His father was a slave. His mother was a free woman who died while he was still very young. Tindley was taken in by an aunt to retain his freedom, but she often hired him out so that he could earn his keep. He taught himself to read and as an adult put himself through school using correspondence courses. Yet for all he had been through, Tindley seemed to have a deep understanding of the purpose of affliction.

His hymn reminds us that our testimonies in heaven will not be about our struggles and suffering. We will tell the stories of how, in Christ, we have overcome. Our stories in heaven will be all about giving God the glory. And we will understand it better by and by.

*Lord, I cannot wait to hear all of the saints
tell their stories around the throne.*

85

I've got the *joy*, joy, joy, joy

Down in my heart (where?)

Down in my heart (where?)

Down in my *heart*;

I've got the joy, joy, joy, joy

Down in *my* heart (where?)

Down in my heart to *stay*.

I'VE GOT THE JOY, JOY, JOY, JOY

Have you ever known someone who exudes joy no matter his or her circumstances? Pastor Alistair Begg once told the story of a man who was battling brain cancer. As he would show up each week for treatments, there was a joy about him. It was so evident that the nurse noted in his chart that the patient was exhibiting "inappropriate joy" considering his circumstances. Perhaps she thought he was in denial or not fully comprehending his situation. But Pastor Begg said, after hearing that story, that it became his life's goal to have inappropriate joy.

Written by George W. Cooke, "I've Got the Joy, Joy, Joy, Joy" has been a favorite in worship services, church camps, and Sunday school classes for decades. You would be hard-pressed to find someone who did not know the lyrics and, possibly, some hand motions to this song. It is a cheerful declaration of a believer's joy that will not come and go based on circumstances. It is a joy that is in our hearts to stay. Happiness can wane depending on what happens to us, but joy comes from Jesus, who never leaves us.

Joy does not mean we are pleased by all of the things that may happen to us. It is not a failure to acknowledge trials or hardships. Joy is a deep, abiding sense of the presence of Jesus and the knowledge that it is all in His hands. No matter what comes your way today, you can have the joy, joy, joy, joy down in your heart.

Lord, give me an inappropriate joy in every circumstance.

86

Have thine *own* way, Lord!
Have thine own way!

Thou art the potter,
I am the *clay*.
Mold me and make
me after thy will,

While I am waiting,
yielded and still.

HAVE THINE OWN WAY, LORD

Adelaide Pollard had a heart for the Lord and for mission work. There was a time in her life when she desired to go to Africa on mission, but she just could not seem to raise the funds necessary for the trip. In a state of distress, she attended a prayer meeting in hopes of encouraging her spirit. While there, an elderly woman prayed, and her prayer so moved Pollard that she penned the hymn "Have Thine Own Way, Lord."

It seems the elderly woman did not pray for any specific blessings in her life or in the lives of those in attendance. Instead she just asked the Lord to have His own way in her life. With those words fresh on her heart and mind, Pollard read the words of the prophet Jeremiah who described himself as the clay and the Lord as the potter (Jeremiah 18:3–4). Before going to bed that night, she had written the lyrics to this song.

We add unnecessary stress and tension in our lives when we insist on clinging to control. There is a freedom and peace that comes when we say, "Have Thine own way, Lord." We can trust Jesus with our futures and with our todays. He knows what our futures hold, and He can handle it all. We only need to wait, be still, and know that He is God.

Lord, I submit to Your leadership
and lordship in my life.

87

It came upon the
midnight clear,

That *glorious*
song of old,

From *angels*
bending near the earth,

To touch their
harps of gold.

IT CAME UPON THE MIDNIGHT CLEAR

At the young age of thirty-seven, Edmund Sears experienced poor physical and mental health, which prevented him from performing the ongoing duties of full-time ministry, and he was therefore forced to retire. He continued to serve part-time at another location, but with so much free time on his hands, Sears turned his attention to literature. Out of his time of darkness came beautiful songs of praise.

He penned "It Came upon the Midnight Clear" during a particularly dark period of depression. Between his personal struggles and world events, Sears painted a picture of a world that could not hear the message of Christmas. It is unique among Christmas carols in that the setting is not Jesus' birth but Sears's own time and place. It was a modern telling of the ancient story.

Sometimes we all need to tell ourselves the Christmas story again. The world is as weary and at war with itself in our day as it was in Edmund Sears's day. There is still sin and strife and a world that needs to hear the angels sing. We are desperately in need of some peace on earth and in our hearts. It's not too late to block out the noise and listen for the heavenly music to float over us once again. Tell us again, Lord, that glorious song of old.

Lord, silence the noise around me
so that I hear only You.

88

When the *storms* of life are raging,

Stand by me (stand by me);

When the storms of *life* are raging,

Stand by me (stand by me);

When the *world* is tossing me

Like a *ship* upon the sea,

Thou Who rulest *wind* and water,

Stand by me (stand by me).

STAND BY ME

Who among us hasn't had someone walk away just when we needed him or her the most? We've all, at some point, been rejected, ignored, uninvited, or unfriended. There's even something called *ghosting* these days. This is where one person ends a relationship without any explanation to the other party and then goes about his or her life as if that relationship never existed. In that kind of world, people are looking for someone who will stand by them.

In his hymn "Stand by Me," Charles Tindley issued a plea for the Lord to be by his side through various seasons of life. The lyrics serve as a perfect prayer outline for anyone who has ever felt tossed about by the world. Tindley wrote to so many specific scenarios that we all have faced or will face one day. He asked for the Lord's presence when life was difficult and when the enemy attacked. He requested His companionship even when the pain was God's own doing. He desired the comfort of the Lord when his body began to fail and he felt like a burden. That pretty much covers all our needs in all of our seasons.

Jesus is faithful when the world is fickle. He stays when everyone else turns away. We will go through all of the scenarios mentioned in Tindley's song, and Jesus will walk with us through it all.

Lord, I'm so grateful that You stand by
me and I never walk alone.

89

Where He may
lead me I will go,

For I have learned
to *trust* Him so,

And I *remember*
'twas for me

That He was slain
on *Calvary*.

I REMEMBER CALVARY

I have made the mistake of navigating through life based on my feelings. Here is what I've discovered: feelings aren't facts. Not only that, but they will often lie to us. That is why Jeremiah—known as the weeping prophet because he felt things deeply—said, "This I recall to my mind, therefore I have hope" (Lamentations 3:21). Jeremiah derived his hope from what he knew and not what he felt.

The same message is found in the hymn "I Remember Calvary." William C. Martin penned the lyrics that pointed to what he knew to be true. He would not give in to doubt or fear because of Calvary. What a great habit for all of us. When we are tempted to worry, we will instead remember what Jesus accomplished on the cross. Anytime we begin to question His love for us, we will remember the sacrifice made on our behalf.

Henry Blackaby once said that he would never question God's love for him. He believed that it was proven on the cross and the subject was settled in his mind. He didn't need any further proof no matter what trials came his way. Oh, that we could feel the same—that we would trust the guidance of God who sacrificed His own Son. When hardships come and the enemy wants us to doubt God's love for us, let's resolve to remember Calvary.

Lord, when I'm scared and cannot see, I
will choose to remember Calvary.

90

Open my *eyes*,
that I may see

Glimpses of truth
Thou hast for me;

Place in my *hands*
the wonderful key

That shall *unclasp*
and set me *free*.

OPEN MY EYES, THAT I MAY SEE

Have you ever struggled to understand Scripture? Maybe you read the words but couldn't seem to grasp the deeper meaning. Or you just felt like you were missing something. It has certainly happened to me. There is good news for those of us who have wanted more insight into God's Word. All we have to do is ask. Wisdom is available to all who desire it (James 1:5).

Clara Scott's hymn "Open My Eyes, That I May See" was based on Psalm 119:18. Although written in the late 1800s, it puts words to the desire of every believer. We all want to know God more intimately and His Word more fully. In that verse, the psalmist asked for the Lord to open his eyes so that he could see and understand God's laws. Scott, in her lyrics, made the same request. Her hymn outlined a few benefits to knowing Scripture, including discerning God's will and being able to distinguish truth from lies.

Two men who struggled to see and understand the truth were the two men walking on the road to Emmaus. They were in the presence of Jesus but failed to understand. However, Jesus opened their eyes and enabled them to truly see Him (Luke 24:31). Whether it's the psalmist, the disciples, Scott, or believers today, the Lord can still open the eyes of those who ask.

> Lord, I want to know Your Word. Open
> my eyes so that I can see.

91

Silent night! *Holy* night!

All is *calm*, all is bright

'Round yon virgin
mother and child.

Holy infant, so *tender*
and mild,

Sleep in *heavenly* peace,

Sleep in heavenly *peace*.

SILENT NIGHT, HOLY NIGHT

Originally written in German, "Silent Night, Holy Night" is the only one of Joseph Mohr's works to be translated into English. It was written for a Christmas Eve service at Mohr's church, but it didn't catch on for a couple of decades. By the middle of the nineteenth century, however, its popularity had spread. Bing Crosby's version of this Christmas classic is the fourth best-selling single of all time. (You really can't go wrong with a Crosby-Christmas combo.)

Over the years, some have questioned the concept of a "silent night" when the song is about a baby being born in a stable. Surely, they claim, there were cries of babe and mother mingled with the noise of various animals. I fear those individuals may have missed the point entirely. It was a silent night in that it was a holy night. There is a stillness in holiness that causes worldly noise to fade into the background.

Take a moment and read the words to Mohr's hymn. Think about it not in terms of a birth story but as God entering the world. Imagine the hush of heaven as all the host held their breath. Envision the awe of the shepherds. See a silent Joseph who just witnessed the Son of God being born. Did a cattle low? Sure. A baby cry? Absolutely. But make no mistake. It was a silent, holy night.

Lord, what a holy night it was when
love came down to earth.

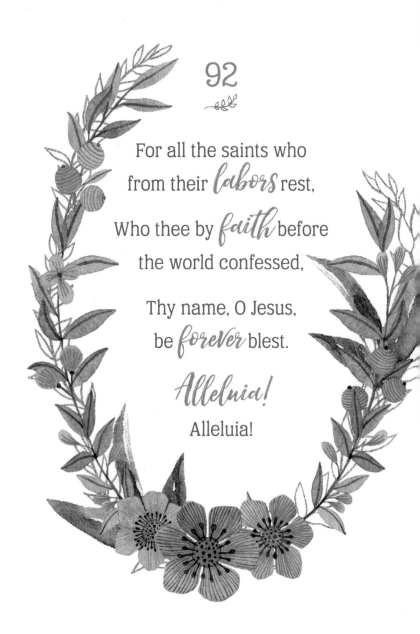

92

For all the saints who
from their *labors* rest,

Who thee by *faith* before
the world confessed,

Thy name, O Jesus,
be *forever* blest.

Alleluia!

Alleluia!

FOR ALL THE SAINTS

William How was deemed the "poor man's bishop" and the "bishop of the children" because of his extensive work among the destitute living in the slums of London. He also served among the lower-income factory workers and spoke up against injustices around him. He wrote approximately sixty hymns, many specifically for children.

"For All the Saints" was an anthem How wrote in honor of those who had fought the good fight. It was for all the saints who were enjoying a rest from their labors as well as fellowship with the Father. It was, at the same time, an encouragement to those still laboring here below. How's hymn reminded believers that one day they, too, would have rest.

The image of all the saints worshiping together brings to mind the image given to John in Revelation 7:9–17. Scripture tells of those who had survived the tribulation and continued to proclaim the name of Christ. They were no longer subject to hunger or thirst. The Lord would wipe every tear from their eyes.

One day we will join the saints in their rest. We will be, as How wrote, one in Christ. We will have finished our race and kept the faith. So when the battle is fierce and the journey is long, we follow our Savior, knowing that He leads us on to victory.

Lord, help me to remain faithful until the day I am counted as one of the saints around Your throne.

93

I have a hope,
Serene and sure,

That *anchors*
past the veil;

In all the storms
it holds *Secure*,

Nor will it
ever fail.

I HAVE A HOPE

Where do you place your hope? Do you hope in your bank account? Your physical appearance? Your education, occupation, or social standing? The problem with any of those things is that they can change at any point in time. Jobs are deleted. Health deteriorates. People walk away. What happens to a person's hope then?

Charles W. Naylor, author of "I Have a Hope," knew exactly the transient nature of earthly sources of hope. While still a young man, Naylor was involved in two severe accidents only a year apart. He was left an invalid for the rest of his life. During those later years, he wrote multiple books, articles, and songs. One of his most well-known pieces was this hymn describing the unshakable hope of the believer.

The author of Hebrews wrote about the sure and steadfast hope we have in Christ (Hebrews 6:19). It isn't dependent upon the ever-changing things of the world but on the eternal, unchanging nature of God. It's the same hope that Naylor described as holding secure in every storm. It is a hope anchored in the Word of God. It focuses not on the things of earth but on the things of heaven. Where is your hope placed today?

Thank You, Lord, for the secure and
steadfast hope we have in You.

94

Joy to the world!
The Lord is come:

Let earth receive her *King*;

Let ev'ry *heart*
prepare Him room,

And heav'n and nature *sing*,

And heav'n and *nature* sing,

And heav'n, and heav'n
and nature sing.

JOY TO THE WORLD

Gifted in learning and literature, Isaac Watts began writing verses as young as age seven. As a teen, he became frustrated with the songs being sung at his local church. The story is told that, after hearing him complain one too many times, Watts's father challenged Isaac to give them something better to sing. Watts accepted the challenge, and he began writing a new hymn for each Sunday. One week, while making his way through the Psalms, Watts wrote "Joy to the World" based on Psalm 98:4. Today there are more versions of "Joy to the World" than any other praise song, with new versions being sung all the time.

The story of Jesus coming to earth was a message of joy to the world. Just imagine—prophets had been pointing forward to the coming of a Messiah. The people had been waiting for generations. The Scriptures told of a time when a Savior would appear. Everything had been building, and suddenly it was time. Joy to the world!

Now we find ourselves waiting with the same anticipation. The Scriptures tell of a time when the Lord will come back. Jesus Himself said that He would be returning for us. We are looking forward to Christ's return to earth. No wonder Watts's song has appealed to so many people for so many years. There really isn't any better way to describe the arrival of Christ than "Joy to the world."

Lord, there will be no greater joy
than the day I see my King.

95

What *man* is this they all did say (They did say)

That the *wind* and seas obey (sea obey)

He's the one who *sails* with me

Oh He's still the *Master* of the *Sea* (of the sea).

MASTER OF THE SEA

It's tempting to read anecdotes in Scripture and minimize the fear the people must have felt during times of trials. We have the luxury of knowing who Jesus was and what He was capable of doing. When the disciples were in a boat on a stormy sea, for instance, the situation was dire.

The hymn "Master of the Sea," written by Southern Gospel singer and songwriter Squire Parsons, is drawn from the story found in Matthew 8, which tells of a harrowing night at sea. The storm was very real, and the boat was overcome with waves. The disciples were afraid because the danger was real. Panic had begun to set in and understandably so.

But then Jesus spoke, and that was all it took. The wind and waves had to obey the One who created them. Whatever happens, the God who spoke everything into existence can still control it all with a word. The waves must calm, and the winds must still.

Whatever storm you're in—financial crisis, marital discord, illness, insecurity, tremendous loss, rocky relationships, search for purpose—your storm has to obey the Lord. Your God is still the Master of the sea.

Lord, all of creation obeys the sound of Your voice.

96

Jesus is all the
world to me,

My *life*,

my joy, my all;

He is my *strength*

from day to day,

Without *Him*

I would fall.

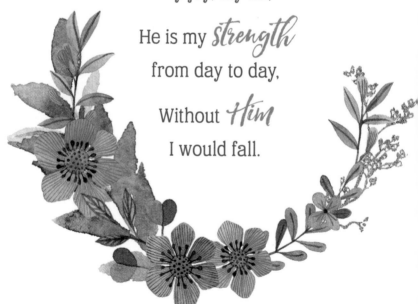

JESUS IS ALL THE WORLD TO ME

Will L. Thompson had a gift for writing songs from a young age. After trying unsuccessfully to sell his songs to a commercial publisher, Thompson simply started his own publishing company. This business later grew to become a retail store that sold pianos, organs, and sheet music. Although he died at a relatively young age, he left behind some beautiful hymns like "Jesus Is All the World to Me."

The lyrics to Thompson's song describe so beautifully what it means to have the Lord as a friend. Friendship with Him entails companionship, encouragement, and comfort. Our Savior is faithful, trustworthy, and steadfast. There is a friend who sticks closer than a brother (Proverbs 18:24), and His name is Jesus.

Maybe you've been let down by friends in the past. Perhaps you've struggled to be understood and accepted. We have all had times when friends weren't what we needed them to be and, if we are honest, times when we were not the friend someone else needed us to be for him. Therein lies the beauty of friendship with Jesus. He will never let us down. And when we let Him down, He is quick to forgive. Jesus is a friend like no other.

> Lord, You are everything to me. I would be
> lost without Your presence in my life.

97

I must *tell* Jesus
all of my trials;

I cannot *bear*
these burdens alone;

In my distress He
kindly will help me;

He ever *loves* and
cares for His own.

I MUST TELL JESUS

If you've ever shared something with the wrong person, then you are aware what poor confidants people can often be. Sometimes they fail to sympathize with what we are going through. Other times they make our personal pains public. A secret shared with the wrong someone can result in a lot of regret. Or maybe you made the mistake of not telling anyone about a struggle, believing that you could handle it on your own. There are some things that no one understands except Jesus.

Elisha Hoffman wrote "I Must Tell Jesus" in 1894. Hoffman served in many churches and chapels around Ohio and is credited with the writing of thousands of gospel songs. We don't know what trials or burdens his lyrics allude to, but we can certainly imagine some of our own while singing them. We have all dealt with discouragement and disappointment, bitterness and betrayal.

Although several verses of Scripture seem to have been on Hoffman's mind as he wrote this hymn, one clear passage is Hebrews 4:15–16. We have a High Priest who understands and sympathizes with our weaknesses. Because of this we can come to Him, boldly approaching His throne, in times of trial or temptation. He, in His compassion, will extend mercy and grace in our time of need. Whatever it is you've been trying to handle on your own, you can tell it to Jesus.

Thank You, Lord, for being a place I can run
to with all my sorrows and celebrations.

98

Come, Thou *Fount*
of ev'ry blessing,

Tune my heart to
sing Thy *grace*;

Streams of mercy,
never ceasing,

Call for songs of
loudest *praise*.

COME, THOU FOUNT OF EVERY BLESSING

"Come, Thou Fount of Every Blessing" was written in 1757 by Robert Robinson, who was a pastor and hymn writer—and was only twenty-two years old at the time. While training to be a hairdresser, Robinson heard a sermon on the judgement day to come. After a spiritual struggle within himself, he chose to pursue a life of ministry.

The lyrics in his hymn have resonated with believers for centuries. Who among us isn't aware of our own heart's propensity to wander and wish that it were not so? We desperately need the grace of God to keep us bound to Him. We want our lives to speak to His goodness and our hearts to sing of His grace.

Samuel promised the people of Israel that, if they would put away their foreign gods and return to God with all their hearts, He would deliver them from the hands of their enemy (1 Samuel 7:3). He will do the same for His people today. We can turn our backs on the false gods we have been serving and return to the One whose mercy never ceases.

Perhaps you have found yourself wandering lately. As long as there's breath in your body, it isn't too late to return to God. His grace is abounding, and His mercies are new every morning. Turn back to Him today.

> Let it be so in our lives, Lord. Tune my
> heart to sing of Your grace.

99

All to Jesus I *surrender*,

All to Him I freely give;

I will ever love and *trust* Him,

In His *presence* daily live.

I SURRENDER ALL

Judson W. Van DeVenter was an art teacher and musician who followed God's calling to become a minister and evangelist. It is said that he struggled greatly for a time trying to choose between his passion for art and the calling he felt to ministry. Finally, Van DeVenter chose to surrender his life to following God's leading. Of the many hymns published in his lifetime, "I Surrender All" is the most famous.

There will come a point in every believer's life when a choice will need to be made between desires and the call of Christ. In Romans 12:1, Paul told the Romans that there is one true and right way to worship God and that is by surrendering our lives—giving all that we are over to Him. "Therefore, I urge you, brothers and sisters, in view of God's mercy, to offer your bodies as a living sacrifice, holy and pleasing to God—this is your true and proper worship" (NIV).

We have all, at some point, felt like we had nothing to offer the Lord. Perhaps we felt like we came before the Lord empty-handed. In reality, we all have something the Lord desires, which is a willing heart. There is work for each person to do no matter what gifts or talents we have to offer. Do we have financial resources? God can use it. Whatever our offering, be it large or small, we can surrender it to Jesus. He never asks or expects something from us that we don't have to give. What pleases God is when we fully surrender ourselves to Him.

Lord, I'm holding nothing back from You.
I surrender all to Your perfect will.

100

This little *light* of mine,

I'm gonna let it *shine*.

This *little* light of mine,

I'm gonna let it shine.

This little light of mine,

I'm gonna *let* it shine,

Let it shine, let it *shine*,

oh let it shine.

THIS LITTLE LIGHT OF MINE

Harold Loes, a music minister from Michigan, may have been responsible for writing 1,500 gospel songs and composing thousands of tunes. But could any of them compare to or be as loved as "This Little Light of Mine"? It is included on the soundtracks of many of our childhoods. Even now you're probably humming the tune under your breath while reading. Written for children in the 1920s, it was given new life when sung during the civil rights movement in the 1960s.

The lyrics seem to resonate with children and adults alike. It is a call for those of us who have the light of Jesus to share that light with the world. We are to let it shine wherever we go and on all the people who cross our paths. Loes's message is simple and one that every Christian understands.

There are people all around us living in darkness. Some are aware of the darkness but don't know how to change it. We have the answer. Still others stumble around and don't even realize that they are in the dark. Are we hoarding and keeping our light to ourselves? Or are we carrying it to all the dark corners of the world? Let's let those little lights shine.

Lord, show me how to shine my
light even brighter for You.

MY FAVORITE HYMNS

_____

_____

_____

_____

_____

_____

_____

_____

_____

_____

_____

_____

_____

_____